Understanding Paganism

*A Beginner's Guide to Embracing Modern
Pagan Beliefs, Practices, and Community*

DAVID M. EATON

Table of Contents

CHAPTER 1

Introduction to Paganism

Welcome to the extraordinary world of Paganism—a spiritual path deeply rooted in nature, lore, and ancient traditions.

For centuries, Paganism has been a source of fascination, misunderstood and undervalued. But now, as the world seeks to reconnect with its spiritual roots, it is the perfect time to rediscover the rich tapestry of Pagan practices, philosophies, and rituals that celebrate the sacredness of every moment and every living being.

This book is designed to serve as a gentle guide for both novices and those well-versed in Paganism, offering a warm invitation to explore ancient wisdom, connect with the divine forces that reside both within and without, and forge a deep, nourishing bond with the natural world.

Through these pages, you will discover a myriad of Pagan traditions, such as Wicca, Druidry, and Shamanism, each offering a unique perspective on the interconnectedness of all things. We will explore the sacred cycles of the sun and moon, the magic of plants and herbs, the power of ritual and spell craft, and how to commune with ancestors and spirit guides.

With an open heart and mind, you will learn how to honor and respect the divine feminine and masculine energies and embrace the beautiful diversity that exists within the Pagan community. Whether seeking personal transformation, a greater sense of belonging, or a deeper connection with the world around you, this book is here to support and inspire you on your own mystical journey.

But first things first, what exactly is Paganism?

What is Paganism?

At its core, Paganism encompasses a range of spiritual traditions and belief systems that honor and celebrate nature, the interconnectedness of all living beings, and the cycles of life. Derived from the Latin word paganus, meaning "country dweller" or "rural folk," Paganism once referred to people living closer to the land, tending to the rhythms of the seasons, and recognizing the sacredness within every facet of existence.

Often misrepresented, Paganism is not a monolithic or dogmatic belief system. Instead, it embraces individuality and diversity, allowing practitioners to forge their own path and define their personal connection to the divine. Paganism thrives on variety, as followers draw inspiration from various ancient and indigenous cultures, folklore, mythology, and nature itself.

Central to Paganism is the recognition and veneration of nature as a living, breathing entity—an interconnectedness that sustains all life. Pagans perceive the natural world as a divine expression, encompassing the elements, plants, animals, and celestial bodies. They embrace the cyclical nature of existence, viewing birth, life, death, and rebirth as interconnected phases intrinsically interwoven with the natural world.

Through rituals, ceremonies, and observances, Pagans seek harmony and balance with nature, nurturing a profound sense of gratitude and reverence for the earth. Whether it be through working with herbs, engaging in outdoor rituals, or celebrating the changing seasons, Pagans find joy in exploring the intricate connections between their own spirituality and the natural world.

Within Paganism, there are several deities, spirits, and divine beings representing various aspects of the natural world, humanity, and the cosmos. Unlike monotheistic traditions, paganism does not encourage the worship of a single supreme deity. Instead, Pagans have the freedom to connect with and honor the deities of their choosing, whether it's Anubis, the Egyptian god of the afterlife, Brigid, the Celtic goddess of healing, or Odin, the Norse god of wisdom.

These deities are often seen as archetypes, embodying certain qualities, lessons, and virtues that followers aspire to emulate. Pagan practices involve offering devotion, seeking guidance, and building personal relationships with the divine, fostering a sense of interconnectedness and partnership.

Why Paganism is Often Misunderstood

Paganism is often misunderstood and subject to misinterpretation. In this section, we will explore the reasons behind this misunderstanding and why it is crucial to learn about Paganism accurately and respectfully. By fostering a deeper understanding, we can break down stereotypes, promote tolerance, and celebrate the richness of human spirituality.

One of the main reasons Paganism is misunderstood is the perpetuation of stereotypes by popular culture, media, and historical biases. These biases often portray Pagans as deluded or somehow dangerous. These misconceptions not only limit our understanding but also create barriers to open dialogue and peaceful coexistence.

Because of this, learning about Paganism is important for creating an inclusive society that respects and celebrates diversity. By exploring the beauty of Paganism, we can shed light on practices rooted in harmony with nature, personal empowerment, and the pursuit of wisdom. This knowledge can help cultivate understanding, empathy, and an appreciation for different belief systems.

To dispel myths and misconceptions, it is vital to approach the study of Paganism with an open mind and a willingness to learn.

Engage in dialogue with practicing Pagans, read reputable books and articles, and attend conferences or workshops. This proactive approach allows for accurate information to replace mistaken assumptions, facilitating a more inclusive and equitable society.

By learning about Paganism with an open heart, we can foster tolerance and acceptance. Understanding the intrinsic value of diverse belief systems can lead to a more harmonious coexistence among individuals of different spiritual backgrounds. Embracing this approach helps us move beyond intolerance and promotes an environment where everyone can freely express their faith without fear of judgment or prejudice.

Overall, Paganism is often misunderstood due to societal biases, stereotypes, and lack of accurate knowledge. By making a conscious effort to learn more about Paganism and engaging in respectful dialogue, we can dismantle misconceptions and embrace diversity.

A Brief History of Paganism

Paganism, often referred to as an umbrella term encompassing a variety of indigenous and nature-based spiritual practices, has a rich and diverse history that spans across centuries and continents.

The roots of Paganism can be traced back to the ancient civilizations that flourished across the globe. In Europe, the Celtic, Norse, and Germanic tribes held strong spiritual beliefs centered around nature, gods, and goddesses. These societies were deeply connected to the rhythms of the natural world and celebrated the cycles of life through seasonal festivals.

During the classical period, various polytheistic religions emerged in different regions. The ancient Greeks worshipped a pantheon of gods and goddesses dwelling on Mount Olympus, while the Romans had their own deities with similar attributes. Egyptian,

Mesopotamian, and other ancient cultures also had their unique pantheons and religious practices.

As Christianity spread throughout Europe, Pagan beliefs faced increasing challenges. The rise of Christianity introduced a monotheistic faith that sought to suppress Pagan practices. The Roman Empire, in particular, viewed Paganism as a threat to its centralized authority and systematically persecuted Pagan practitioners.

Despite centuries of oppression, Pagan traditions managed to survive in the background of European societies. However, it was during the 19th and 20th centuries that Paganism experienced a significant revival. Inspired by archaeological discoveries, literature, folklore, and a growing interest in spirituality beyond mainstream religions, various Pagan movements emerged.

Wicca, one of the most well-known forms of modern Paganism, was established in the mid-20th century by Gerald Gardner. Drawing upon ancient European traditions, Wicca emphasized the veneration of the divine feminine, nature worship, and a reverence for the cycles of the moon. Other contemporary Pagan traditions include Druidry, Heathenry, Ásatrú, and various Earth-centered spiritual paths.

Contemporary Paganism today encompasses a wide array of beliefs and practices, often focusing on honoring nature, nurturing personal relationships with deities or spirits, and celebrating the interconnectedness of all living things. It has gained recognition as a legitimate spiritual path in many countries, fostering communities and promoting environmental stewardship, equality, and personal growth.

Diversity Within Paganism

In Paganism, diversity is not only celebrated, but it is at the very heart of the religion. The Pagan community thrives on the beauty and richness that comes from embracing a wide range of beliefs, practices, traditions, and cultures. One of the greatest strengths of Paganism is its ability to accommodate and incorporate diverse perspectives, making it a truly inclusive and welcoming spiritual path.

Diversity can be observed in a multitude of ways. First and foremost, there is a vast array of Pagan belief systems, each with its own unique set of deities, rituals, and practices. From Wicca to Druidry, from Heathenry to Asatru, and from Hellenismos to Eclectic Paganism, there is no shortage of paths to explore and connect with.

Furthermore, Paganism embraces diversity in terms of individual spiritual experiences. Each person is encouraged to develop their own personal connection with the divine, allowing for a deeply individualized and subjective understanding of spirituality. This means that no two Pagans will have the exact same relationship with their deities or approach to magic and ritual, fostering a combination of perspectives within the community.

Moreover, Paganism is immensely diverse in its cultural and ethnic range. It draws inspiration from ancient civilizations across the globe, including but not limited to Celtic, Norse, Greek, Roman, Egyptian, Native American, and African traditions. This cultural diversity enriches the collective pool of knowledge and wisdom within Paganism, offering followers the opportunity to learn from and honor a wide range of ancestral traditions.

In addition to cultural diversity, Paganism embraces people from all walks of life, regardless of gender, sexual orientation, age, ability, or socioeconomic background. It is a religion that values and respects the inherent worth and dignity of every individual, fostering an environment that encourages personal growth, self-expression, and acceptance. Pagans often prioritize social justice and activism, recognizing that fostering a diverse and inclusive community is an integral part of their spiritual path.

Overall, the diversity within Paganism allows for a multifaceted and eclectic approach to spirituality. It encourages followers to continually explore, learn, and engage with different traditions, creating an inclusive and ever-evolving spiritual landscape. By embracing and celebrating diversity, Paganism cultivates a global community that values the beauty of individuality and the power of collective unity.

CHAPTER 2

The Foundations of Pagan Beliefs

U nderstanding the basics of Paganism allows us to open our minds and really explore the beauty of this belief system. As we know, Paganism is often misunderstood and seen as something dark or even dangerous. However, once you delve into the beliefs that make up Paganism, you'll see that it's far from the truth.

At the heart of Paganism lies nature, and it presses forth the idea that we are all stewards for the planet we live on. As such, we should respect everything within the natural world and treat it with kindness and generosity.

In this chapter, we will delve further into the basic Pagan beliefs, as well as learning more about the deities, texts, and traditions.

The Concept of Nature Spirituality

In today's fast-paced, technology-driven society, many people seek solace and connection to something greater than themselves. Paganism, a spiritual path that nourishes a deep connection with nature, offers seekers a unique and profound way to experience spirituality.

At the heart of Paganism lies the concept of nature spirituality, a belief system that celebrates and reveres the natural world as a manifestation of the divine.

Nature spirituality in Paganism is grounded in the belief that the earth and all its elements possess inherent spiritual qualities. Pagans view nature as a living, interconnected web of life that deserves respect, care, and reverence. They see the Divine as immanent in the natural world, manifesting in trees, rivers, mountains, animals, and every living being. Through this perspective, Pagans find beauty, wisdom, and inspiration in the cycles of the seasons, the changing phases of the moon, and the intricate interconnectedness of all living things.

For Pagans, nature spirituality holds immense significance on several levels. First and foremost, it serves as a reminder of our interconnectedness with all beings. Paganism espouses the belief that humans are not separate from nature but rather an integral part of it. By recognizing this connection, Pagans develop a deep sense of responsibility toward nature, nurturing a desire to protect and live harmoniously with the environment.

Nature spirituality also helps Pagans find meaning and purpose in their lives. Through observing the cycles of nature, Pagans see reflections of their own experiences—the ebb and flow, growth and decay, birth, and death. This recognition of the natural rhythms of life brings about a sense of balance and equanimity. It helps followers navigate their own individual journeys, reminding them that life, like nature, is cyclical and ever-changing.

In order to cultivate nature spirituality, Pagans engage in a variety of practices that deepen their connection with the natural world. One such practice is nature observation and meditation. By spending time in nature, Pagans attune themselves to the subtle rhythms and energies of the environment. They observe the behavior of animals, the blooming of flowers, and the movement of the wind, allowing these experiences to evoke a sense of wonder and inspiration. Through meditation, Pagans quiet the mind and open themselves up to the wisdom and guidance that nature has to offer.

Another important practice in nature spirituality is ritual and ceremony. By engaging in sacred rituals, followers honor the natural world and establish a sacred space in which they can commune with the Divine. These rituals can range from simple acts of gratitude, such as offering food or water to the earth, to more elaborate ceremonies that celebrate the changing of the seasons. By partaking in these rituals, Pagans seek to align themselves with the natural cycles of life, fostering a deep sense of connection and harmony.

The Role of Deities in Paganism

Paganism encompasses a wide range of spiritual beliefs that honor nature, the earth, and various gods and goddesses. Unlike monotheistic religions, which worship a single supreme deity, Paganism embraces a polytheistic approach where multiple deities are acknowledged and worshiped. These deities represent different aspects of existence, each with their own unique characteristics, powers, and domains.

These ancient gods and goddesses span across various pantheons and cultures, representing different aspects of nature, life, love, and power. Here are some of the most significant:

- **Gaia (Mother Earth):** Gaia, deriving from ancient Greek mythology, personifies the earth itself. She is the embodiment of the planet's fertility, nurturing and sustaining all life forms on it. Gaia teaches about interconnectedness, reminding us to treat the earth with reverence and gratitude.

- **Odin (Allfather):** In Norse mythology, Odin is the chief god and ruler of Asgard. Known as the Allfather, he is associated with wisdom, knowledge, and warfare. Odin's quest for wisdom led him to sacrifice one of his eyes, symbolizing the value of sacrifice for the greater good. He encourages wisdom and inner strength in life.

- **Aphrodite (Goddess of Love):** Associated with beauty, love, and desire, Aphrodite is a prominent deity in Greek mythology. She represents the power and allure of love in all its forms, including romantic love, friendship, and self-love. Aphrodite teaches about embracing love within and creating harmonious connections with others.

- **Cernunnos (Horned God):** Cernunnos, often depicted with antlers or horns, is an ancient Celtic deity associated with nature, fertility, and the cycle of life and death. As the guardian of the wilderness and animals, he encourages followers to honor and protect the environment.

- **Bastet (Goddess of Protection):** Hailing from ancient Egyptian mythology, Bastet is a lioness-headed goddess associated with protection, fertility, and playfulness. She is known as both a fierce protector and a nurturing presence. Bastet encourages followers to embrace their own inner strength and to find joy and balance in their lives.

These deities are just a glimpse into the many Pagan gods and goddesses, each providing their own unique insights and blessings.

Deities are seen as divine beings who possess immense wisdom, guidance, and the ability to influence the natural world. They are not distant or detached from human affairs, but rather actively involved in the lives of their followers. They are viewed as companions, allies, and sources of inspiration and empowerment. The deities in Paganism are also often associated with specific natural elements, such as rivers, trees, animals, or celestial bodies, emphasizing the interconnectedness between the spiritual realm and the natural world.

One of the significant roles of deities is that they serve as guardians and protectors of the earth and its inhabitants. Each deity is associated with different aspects of nature, such as agriculture, fertility, the seasons, or the ocean. By recognizing and honoring these deities, Pagans aim to establish a harmonious relationship with nature and maintain a balance in the ecosystems they inhabit. It is believed that by showing respect and gratitude to the deities, humans can maintain this balance, ensuring the fertility of the land, the abundance of resources, and the overall well-being of the community.

Deities in Paganism are also revered as teachers and guides. They possess immense knowledge and wisdom, which they share with their followers in various ways, such as through myths, legends, or personal spiritual experiences. By studying the stories and teachings associated with each deity, Pagans gain insights into different aspects of life and develop a deeper understanding of themselves and their place in the world. These teachings often emphasize the importance of living in harmony with nature, fostering community connections, and practicing self-reflection and personal growth.

Furthermore, deities play a crucial role in ritual and spell work. They are invoked and called upon during ceremonies, rituals, and magical practices. Pagans believe that by establishing a connection with specific deities, they can draw upon their energy and assistance to manifest their intentions and desires. Each deity possesses distinct qualities and powers that can be utilized for different purposes, such as healing, protection, fertility, or creativity. Through prayer, offerings, meditation, and various rituals, Pagans seek to establish a relationship with these deities, seeking their aid and guidance in navigating life's challenges and celebrating life's joys.

Another essential aspect of deities in Paganism is the concept of personal relationships and connections. Unlike in some organized religions, where the relationship between the divine and the followers is mediated by religious figures, Pagans believe in direct and personal connections with deities. This means that each individual practitioner may have their own unique relationship with one or multiple deities. These relationships are built upon mutual respect, trust, and ongoing communication. This personal connection allows for a deep understanding of the deity's nature, guidance tailored to the individual's needs, and a sense of companionship and support.

Sacred Texts and Oral Traditions in Paganism

In Paganism, the transmission of religious knowledge and spirituality is often carried out through a combination of sacred texts and oral traditions. These elements play a significant role in the diverse and vibrant cocktail of Pagan belief systems.

Sacred texts in Paganism encompass a wide range of sources, drawing inspiration from ancient myths, folklore, and historical records. These texts often serve as a guide to understanding the cosmology, ethics, and rituals of various Pagan traditions. However, unlike in some other religious practices where there is a singular authoritative text, Paganism embraces a more fluid and decentralized approach.

Therefore, there is no single set of universally accepted sacred texts like in some other religions. However, there are numerous important texts and traditions that hold spiritual significance to various Pagan paths. Here are a few examples:

- **Wicca:** Many Wiccans consider the "Book of Shadows" as a personal sacred text. It contains rituals, spells, and spiritual guidance specific to each individual practitioner or coven.

- **Druidry:** "The Mabinogion" is a collection of Welsh myths and legends that hold significance for Druids. It is a rich source of wisdom and inspiration.

- **Norse Paganism:** The "Poetic Edda" and the "Prose Edda" are essential texts for followers of Norse Paganism. They contain myths, poetry, and narratives about Norse gods, heroes, and history.

- **Hellenism:** In Hellenic Paganism, sacred texts include the Homeric Hymns, the works of philosophers like Plato, and the "Odyssey" and the "Iliad" by Homer.

- **Heathenry:** Heathens may refer to texts like the "Havamal" (part of the Poetic Edda) and the "Prose Edda" for guidance on ethical and moral principles.

We can find sacred texts in Paganism from different cultures and time periods, such as the Eddas in Norse Paganism, the Celtic myths, the Greek and Roman pantheons, and the Wiccan Book of Shadows. These texts may vary in their level of preservation and historical accuracy, but they provide a rich source of inspiration and insight for Pagans seeking to understand their spiritual heritage.

In addition to written texts, oral traditions have long played a crucial role in the transmission of Pagan knowledge. These oral traditions are often passed down from one generation to the next through storytelling, songs, chants, and rituals. Through oral traditions, wisdom, practices, and mythologies, Paganism is kept alive and preserved within Pagan communities.

The use of oral traditions in Paganism allows for the flexibility and adaptability of beliefs and practices within different contexts. They create a dynamic and living spiritual tradition that can evolve and grow alongside the needs and experiences of the community. This flexibility also fosters a sense of communal participation, as individuals have the opportunity to contribute their own experiences and interpretations to the oral traditions.

It is important to note that Paganism values personal experience and direct connection with divinity. This emphasis on individual spirituality and exploration often encourages practitioners to trust their own intuition and inner guidance. This aspect of Paganism complements the use of both sacred texts and oral traditions, providing a balance between established knowledge and personal spiritual connections.

CHAPTER 3

Exploring Pagan Practices

F rom the enchanting ceremonies of Beltane, where fires are lit to rejuvenate the land and kindle passion within hearts, to the reverent observances of Samhain, when the veil between worlds thins and we honor our ancestors, Pagan practices carry a profound sense of reverence and connection.

In this chapter, we will delve into the practices of divination, spell craft, and rituals that form the core of Pagan traditions. We will explore the versatility of crystals in harnessing unique energies, the art of tarot and oracle cards to gain deep insights, and the power of herbs and oils in creating potions and remedies.

It is these practices that often cause a level of misunderstanding over what Paganism is, however, that is often rooted in a lack of knowledge. Through learning about these rituals and ceremonies, we can seek to deepen our understanding and celebrate the beauty of this ancient belief system.

Pagan Rituals and Ceremonies

Pagan rituals and ceremonies hold significant importance in connecting followers with the natural world, honoring deities, and celebrating the cycles of nature. Let's delve into some of the most important rituals and ceremonies performed within Paganism.

Sabbats

Sabbats are seasonal celebrations that mark the turning points of the yearly cycle. There are eight Sabbats in total, four major and four minor. The major Sabbats are the solstices and equinoxes, which include Yule (winter solstice), Ostara (spring equinox), Litha (summer solstice), and Mabon (autumn equinox).

The minor Sabbats represent the points between the solstices and equinoxes and include Imbolc, Beltane, Lammas, and Samhain. These celebrations often involve gatherings, feasting, music, dancing, and rituals specific to each season, such as lighting bonfires or decorating altars with seasonal offerings.

Esbats

Esbats are monthly rituals performed during the Full Moon and, in some cases, the New Moon. These gatherings provide an opportunity for Pagans to honor and connect with the lunar energy.

Esbats generally involve communing with the Moon through meditation, chanting, spell work, divination, and offerings made to lunar deities. Some practitioners choose to conduct their divination rituals during Esbats, as they believe the Moon's energy enhances their connection to their intuition and the spiritual realm.

Handfasting

Handfasting is a Pagan wedding ceremony that symbolizes the union of two individuals. This ritual can be as simple or elaborate as the couple desires, but it typically involves exchanging vows, exchanging rings or other symbolic objects, and binding their hands together with a cord or ribbon.

Handfasting ceremonies embrace the Pagan belief in the cyclical nature of relationships and the idea that love, and commitment can wax and wane like the phases of the Moon. Handfasting can be performed in a variety of settings, such as forests, beaches, or sacred groves, and often incorporate elements of nature, like flowers, foliage, or stones.

Rites of Passage

Paganism acknowledges various stages and transitions within an individual's life, marking these milestones with specific rites of passage. Birth blessings or welcoming ceremonies celebrate the arrival of a new life, incorporating elements of protection, guidance, and community support.

Coming-of-age rituals honor the transition from childhood to adulthood, acknowledging the individual's newfound responsibilities and abilities. Handparting ceremonies, or Pagan divorces, provide a formal process for ending a relationship with respect and gratitude for shared experiences. Transitioning ceremonies celebrate gender identity and help individuals on their path to self-discovery and self-acceptance.

Harvest Festivals

Similar to the concept of Thanksgiving, Pagan harvest festivals celebrate the abundance of the earth and give thanks for the bountiful harvest. These ceremonies typically take place during the autumnal equinox and are known by different names across Pagan traditions, such as Mabon, Lammas, or Harvest Home.

The rituals involve offerings of fruits, vegetables, grains, and other seasonal produce, as well as prayers or chants expressing gratitude for the earth's generosity and the interconnectedness of all living beings.

Ancestor Veneration

Many Pagans honor their ancestors through rituals and ceremonies that acknowledge the wisdom, guidance, and support passed down through generations. Ancestor rituals often involve setting up an ancestral altar with pictures, mementos, or symbols representing the deceased loved ones.

Rituals may include calling upon ancestral spirits for guidance, expressing gratitude for their presence in one's life, lighting candles, and offering food or drink as a symbolic gesture of remembrance.

These are just a few examples of the many diverse rituals and ceremonies within Paganism. Each tradition and individual practitioner may have unique practices, beliefs, and rituals, influenced by their personal connection to nature, ancestry, and spirituality. Pagan rituals and ceremonies serve as celebrations of life, an opportunity to connect with the divine, and a means to foster unity and harmony within the natural and supernatural realms.

Pagan Symbols and Their Meanings

Central to Paganism is the use of symbols, which hold deep meanings and serve as powerful tools for spiritual expression. Let's explore some widely recognized Pagan symbols, their meanings, how they are used, and what they signify to practitioners.

The Pentacle

The pentacle is one of the most recognizable and widely used symbols in Paganism. It consists of a pentagram enclosed within a circle. The five points of the pentagram typically represent the four elements (earth, air, fire, and water) and the fifth point, spirit.

The circle symbolizes unity, wholeness, and protection. Pagans often wear or display the pentacle as an amulet or talisman, invoking its protective properties and connection to the natural world.

Pagans utilize the pentacle as a potent symbol imbued with various meanings and purposes. It is often used as a protective talisman, harnessing its powers to ward off negative energies and promote spiritual growth. It is commonly employed in rituals and ceremonies, acting as a focal point for channeling energy and intentions. Additionally, the pentacle serves as a visual reminder of the harmony between nature and divinity, reinforcing the Pagan beliefs in the sacredness of all life and the cycles of the natural world.

Triple Moon Symbol

The triple moon symbol, also known as the triple goddess symbol, is a representation of the phases of the moon (waxing, full, and waning). This symbolizes the cycles of life, death, and rebirth, as well as the triple aspect of the goddess: maiden, mother, and crone.

In Pagan traditions, the symbol is strongly associated with the Triple Goddess, which signifies the three main phases of a woman's life: the maiden, the mother, and the crone. Each phase represents different aspects of femininity, symbolizing youth, fertility, wisdom, and transformation. Pagans may incorporate the triple moon symbol in their rituals, altars, and even as jewelry to honor the goddess and to invoke its qualities.

Triquetra

The triquetra is a Celtic knot symbol with three interlocking loops. It is associated with the concept of unity and continuity, representing elements such as past, present, and future; earth, sea, and sky; or body, mind, and spirit.

Pagans utilize the triquetra as a symbol of wholeness, balance, and interconnectedness. It is often integrated into rituals, artwork, or jewelry as a visual reminder of the harmonious integration of various aspects of existence.

Tree of Life

The Tree of Life symbol holds significant meaning across multiple religions and belief systems, including Paganism. Its roots represent the connection to the earth, its branches reaching up to the heavens, and its trunk serving as the bridge between the two realms.

In Paganism, the Tree of Life is seen as a sacred and powerful symbol of balance, growth, and spiritual evolution. It embodies the interconnectedness of all living beings and the cycle of life and death.

Pagans often incorporate the tree of life symbol into their rituals, using it as a focal point for meditation, visualization, and energy work. It is also commonly utilized in sacred art, jewelry, and tattoos as a way to carry the essence of this profound symbol with them and honor their spiritual beliefs. The tree of life symbol invites Pagans to reflect on their own personal growth and journey, while fostering a sense of unity and harmony with the web of life that surrounds them.

Cauldron

The cauldron holds a special place in Pagan rituals and practices. It represents the womb of the Goddess, symbolizing birth, transformation, and rebirth. In ancient times, cauldrons were used for cooking and brewing potions, making them a potent symbol of creativity and the transformative power of the divine feminine.

Today, the cauldron is often used in rituals to hold offerings, incense, or sacred herbs and is deemed an essential tool for energy work and spell casting.

Sun and Moon Symbols

The sun and moon are common Pagan symbols, usually representing the masculine (sun) and feminine (moon) energies, respectively.

Pagans hold the sun and moon symbols in high regard, recognizing their immense significance in spiritual and magical practices. The sun represents warmth, light, and life-giving energy, symbolizing vitality, strength, and the masculine energy. Pagans often honor the sun during solstices and equinoxes, celebrating the cycles of nature and the changing seasons.

On the other hand, the moon embodies feminine energy, intuition, and the mystical realms. Pagans follow lunar cycles closely, using the moon's phases to guide their rituals, spell work, and divination practices. The moon's waxing and waning are seen as symbolic of personal growth and transformation, reflecting the ebb and flow of life's energies. For Pagans, the sun and moon symbols serve as a constant reminder of the interconnectedness between nature, spirituality, and the cycles of life itself.

As you can see, Pagan symbols are not just mere aesthetic patterns, but powerful tools that hold deep significance within Paganism. They serve as a visual language, evoking spiritual connections, and embodying diverse meanings.

Tools of the Trade: Athames, Wands, and Altars

Within Paganism, various tools are employed to aid in rituals, spellcasting, and spiritual connection. Athames, wands, and altars are among the fundamental tools used, each carrying a unique symbolic meaning and serving distinct purposes.

In this section, let's explore these ancient tools, their significance, how they are used, and why they hold a special place in the practice of Paganism.

The Athame

Athames hold a prominent position among the tools of Paganism. Essentially, an athame is a ceremonial dagger with a double-edged blade and a traditionally black handle. The word "athame" is derived from the Old English word "atham," meaning "to harm" or "to strike." However, in the context of Paganism, the athame is never used for physical harm; it is considered a powerful instrument for directing energy and intention.

The athame symbolizes the masculine aspect of divinity, possessing the qualities of strength, focus, and power. It is often associated with the element of fire in rituals and is believed to carry the spirit of the divine masculine within it. Athames are often consecrated and personalized by their wielders, becoming embodiments of the practitioner's energy.

Athames are primarily used to direct energy in various ceremonies, including casting circles, cutting a doorway between dimensions, invoking, or banishing, and drawing upon the energy of the practitioner. The blade is also used to symbolically inscribe symbols or sigils on candles or other ritual objects. Through the use of an athame, Pagans establish a connection with the divine, their intention magnified through this sacred tool.

The Wand

Wands have long been associated with magic and mysticism, and their presence within Paganism is no exception. A wand is a length of wood or other material that is often decorated and imbued with personal symbolism. Wands are seen as extensions of the witch's or practitioner's energy and can be regarded as a conduit for performing magic.

The wand represents the feminine aspect of divinity, embodying qualities of intuition, creativity, and manipulation of energy. In mythology, wands are often associated with the ancient Greek goddess Hecate and the Celtic god Cernunnos, both symbolizing the power of magic and transformation. Wands are believed to hold the energy of the practitioner and facilitate a deeper connection with the spiritual realms.

Wands are used in various rituals, such as casting circles, invoking, or banishing energies, and directing energy during spellcasting. The wand can be used to draw magical symbols in the air, bless objects, or channel energy from the practitioner's hands. By holding and utilizing a wand, Pagans direct their intentions and harness the energy of nature and the divine into their magical workings.

The Altar

At the heart of many Pagan practices lies the altar, a central and cherished feature of rituals and spellcasting. An altar can be as simple as a cleared space or as elaborate as a dedicated piece of furniture adorned with symbolic objects.

The altar serves as a focal point for worshipping, connecting with the divine, and calling upon the energies associated with specific intentions. It is the physical representation of the Pagan's spiritual journey, creating a sacred space where the realms of the divine and the mundane meet. Altars often incorporate representations of the elements, such as candles, stones, water, and air, providing a connection to the forces of nature.

Altars are used in various Pagan rituals, such as seasonal celebrations, moon rituals, and spellcasting. They are also personal spaces where practitioners can place offerings, sacred objects, and tools specific to their practice. Altars act as an anchor for focusing one's thoughts, intentions, and energy toward spiritual growth and connection with the divine.

These tools each imbued with unique symbolism and purpose and play significant roles in the rituals and practices of Pagans. Understanding the importance of these tools encourages a deeper appreciation of the spiritual journeys traveled by those who practice Paganism.

CHAPTER 4

Types of Paganism

From Wicca and Druidry to Asatru and Hellenismos, the different types of Paganism encompass a broad spectrum of ancient and modern spiritual paths. While these paths may seem distinct on the surface, they share an underlying foundation rooted in animism, earth-centric spirituality, and a deep reverence for the divine in all its forms.

What is truly remarkable about Paganism is how these various strands, seemingly disparate in nature, weave together to create a beautiful and interconnected whole. They do not compete or clash, but rather complement and enrich one another, much like a tapestry woven with carefully chosen colors and patterns.

Despite their differences, Pagan traditions find common ground in their reverence for nature and the cycles of life. Whether it's the celebration of the wheel of the year, the worship of deities representing natural forces, or the deep connection to sacred places, the threads of Paganism are intricately bound to the natural world.

Moreover, Paganism offers a combination of personal spiritual experiences that allows individuals to tailor their path to their unique beliefs and inclinations. Some may find solace in the rituals and magical practices of Wicca, while others may feel a deep resonance with the ancestral wisdom of Heathenry. Regardless of the chosen path, all are welcomed and encouraged to explore, grow, and connect with the divine forces that resonate within them.

There are many different types of Paganism that are celebrated across the world, including:

- **Wicca:** Wicca is a modern Pagan witchcraft tradition that focuses on nature-based spirituality and reverence for the Goddess and God. Wiccans often incorporate rituals, spell work, and the celebration of seasonal cycles known as Sabbats.

- **Druidry:** Druidry draws inspiration from Celtic spirituality and ancient practices attributed to the druids. It emphasizes a deep connection with nature, wisdom, and the pursuit of knowledge. Druids often hold rituals outdoors and celebrate the cycles of the sun and the earth.

- **Heathenry:** Heathenry, also known as Ásatrú or Norse Paganism, follows the ancient Germanic and Scandinavian beliefs. Devotees of this tradition honor the Norse gods and goddesses, such as Odin, Thor, and Freyja. Rituals often involve the use of runes, Norse sagas, and the cycles of the seasons.

- **Asatru:** This branch of Heathenry focuses specifically on the worship of the Norse gods and goddesses, emphasizing the reconstruction of ancient Norse traditions and mythology.

- **Hellenism:** Also referred to as Hellenic Paganism or Hellenismos, this path involves the worship of the ancient Greek gods and goddesses, such as Zeus, Athena, and Aphrodite. It emphasizes virtue, knowledge, and the practice of rituals like libations and sacrifices.

- **Eclectic Paganism:** Eclectic Pagans draw inspiration from a variety of Pagan traditions and incorporate different beliefs and practices into their own spiritual path. This allows them to tailor their practice according to their personal preferences and what resonates with them most.

- **Shamanism:** Shamanism is a spiritual practice found in different cultures around the world. It involves connecting with the spirit world, journeying, and working with spirits, guides, and animal allies for healing and guidance.

- **Traditional Witchcraft:** Traditional Witchcraft refers to various pre-modern European folk magic practices. It often involves working with herbs, spells, divination, and honoring ancestral spirits.

- **Norse Paganism:** As mentioned earlier, Norse Paganism, or Heathenry, is a specific branch of Paganism that focuses on the old Norse deities, myths, and traditions.

- **Celtic Paganism:** This path encompasses several different traditions from various Celtic cultures, such as Irish, Scottish, Welsh, or Gaulish Paganism. It involves honoring Celtic deities, folklore, and sacred sites.

Despite all of these types, the three most commonly followed are Wicca, Druidry, and Heathenry. So, let's explore those in more detail.

Wicca: Origins, Beliefs, and Practices

Wicca, often referred to as Pagan Witchcraft, is a modern religious movement deeply rooted in ancient traditions. With its focus on nature reverence, feminist ideals, and magical practices, Wicca has captured the fascination of many people seeking a more spiritually connected and harmonious existence.

The origins of Wicca can be traced back to mid-20th century England with the establishment of the modern witchcraft movement by Gerald Gardner. Inspired by diverse sources such as Western occultism, Freemasonry, Celtic mythology, and Romanticism, Wicca emerged as a magical and earth-centered religion.

Gardner claimed that he was initiated into an existing witchcraft coven and based his practices on their rituals and beliefs. However, historical evidence regarding the direct lineage of Wicca remains scarce, leading some to consider it more as a modern reinvention of ancient Pagan traditions.

Wiccan Beliefs

At its core, Wicca embraces a pantheistic worldview, considering divinity to be immanent within nature. This belief system acknowledges a multitude of deities, both male and female, with the primary deity often represented as a Goddess and a God. These encompass various traditions such as Celtic, Greek, Egyptian, and Norse, each with their unique pantheon. Wiccans deeply respect and honor nature, seeing it as sacred and divine, with rituals often coinciding with the cycles of the moon and the seasons.

Wiccans embrace the concept of the Wiccan Rede, often summarized as "An it harm none, do what ye will." This encourages adherents to follow their own path as long as it doesn't cause harm to themselves or others. A central ethical principle within Wicca is the Threefold Law, which states that whatever energy or actions you put forth into the universe will return to you threefold.

Practices of Wicca

Ritual practices are essential to Wicca, providing a means for connecting with the divine, celebrating nature, and manifesting intentions. These rites are usually conducted in sacred spaces known as "circles" or "groves," which are energetically cleansed and consecrated prior to each ritual. Many Wiccans choose to work in covens, which are small groups of like-minded practitioners, while others prefer to practice as solitaries.

The Wheel of the Year, a series of eight festivals also known as Sabbats, plays a significant role in Wiccan observances. These celebrations mark the seasons and agricultural cycles, honoring the waxing and waning of the sun's power. The most widely recognized Sabbats are Samhain, Imbolc, Beltane, and Lammas. Additionally, Wiccans pay homage to the lunar cycles through Esbats, which typically occur during the full moon and are specific to cultivating magical energy and spiritual connection.

The use of magic, spells, and divination is another prominent aspect of Wiccan practice. Drawing upon the energetic forces of the universe, Wiccans embrace spell work as a means of manifesting their desires, promoting healing, and enhancing spiritual growth. Divination tools like tarot cards, runes, and scrying mirrors are often employed to seek guidance and insight into the future.

Prevalence of Wicca

Estimating the exact number of Wiccans worldwide is challenging due to the decentralized and individualistic nature of the faith. However, it is safe to say that Wicca has gained significant popularity and acceptance since its emergence in the mid-20th century. With its emphasis on personal empowerment, reverence for nature, and emphasis on ritual, Wicca continues to attract adherents from diverse backgrounds seeking spiritual fulfillment.

Although Wicca is most commonly practiced in English-speaking countries such as the United States, Canada, and the United Kingdom, Wiccan communities can be found around the globe. Many practitioners maintain active participation in online communities and social networks, sharing knowledge, experiences, and fostering a sense of support and belonging.

Druidry: Nature-Based Spirituality and Reverence for Ancestors

Druidry, often referred to as Druidism, is an ancient spiritual practice that holds a deeply rooted connection to nature and a profound reverence for ancestors. While its origins go back centuries, modern Druidry has gained popularity as people seek a spiritual path that engages them with the natural world. With a focus on environmental stewardship and honoring one's cultural heritage, Druidry offers a unique approach to spirituality that resonates with a growing number of individuals today.

Druidry traces its roots to the ancient Celtic tradition, primarily associated with the British Isles and Gaul (modern-day France). As the spiritual leaders, advisors, and healers of their communities, Druids played a vital role in Celtic society. They were highly regarded as intermediaries between the natural and supernatural world, responsible for conducting rituals, preserving knowledge, and maintaining moral and ethical standards.

Nature-Based Spirituality

At the heart of Druidry lies a deep connection and reverence for the natural world. Nature is considered sacred, and Druids strive to establish and renew their relationship with it. Observing the cycles of the seasons, working with plants and animals, and respecting the inherent interconnectedness of all life forms are central aspects of Druidic practice. By immersing themselves in nature, Druids seek spiritual inspiration, guidance, and healing.

Reverence for Ancestors

Druidry also places significant importance on honoring and connecting with one's ancestors. Ancestors are seen as important guides and mentors who offer wisdom and support from the spirit realm.

Druids believe that by cultivating a relationship with their ancestors, they can gain a deeper understanding of their own cultural heritage and a sense of belonging within a broader lineage. Ancestral rituals, storytelling, and researching family histories are common practices within Druidic traditions.

Practices

Druidic practices encompass a range of rituals, ceremonies, and observances. Some common practices include:

- **Natural celebrations:** Druids mark the changing of the seasons with elaborate ceremonies known as the eight festivals, or Sabbats. These celebrations, such as Samhain, Beltane, and Imbolc, are based on the agricultural and astronomical cycles and provide opportunities for connection with nature.

- **Meditation and divination:** Druids often engage in meditative practices to deepen their connection with the natural world and seek guidance from their ancestors or deities. Divination, such as reading omens or using tarot cards, is used to gain insight and clarity.

- **Rituals of healing:** Druids utilize various healing practices, such as herbalism, energy work, and shamanic journeying. They believe in the interconnectedness of mind, body, and spirit and strive to support well-being on all levels.

Heathenry: Norse Paganism and Honoring the Gods of Old

Heathenry, also known as Germanic Neopaganism or Heathenism, is a modern-day revival of the ancient Germanic, Norse, and Anglo-Saxon religious traditions. It is a polytheistic and earth-centered belief system that honors the gods and goddesses of old.

Heathenry traces its roots to the pre-Christian religious practices of the Germanic peoples, including the Norse, Germanic, and Anglo-Saxon tribes. These indigenous traditions were prevalent in Northern Europe before the widespread adoption of Christianity.

After centuries of Christian dominance, interest in these ancient belief systems was revived in the late 19th and early 20th centuries.

The revival was fueled by a desire to connect with ancestral heritage, cultural identity, and a longing for a spiritual connection to nature.

Beliefs

Heathenry encompasses a wide range of beliefs and interpretations, as there is no central authority or dogma. However, some common core beliefs can be identified. Heathens generally believe in a pantheon of gods and goddesses who are seen as divine beings with distinct personalities, mythologies, and domains of influence. These deities include figures such as Odin, Thor, Freya, and Loki, among others. The gods are revered and seen as allies and guides, but not necessarily all-powerful or infallible.

Heathenry often values a strong connection to nature and reveres the land, the spirits of the land, and the ancestors. Ancestor worship and ancestral veneration play an integral role in many Heathen practices. This belief system emphasizes personal responsibility, individual honor, and the importance of community, known as the Kindred. The Kindred is a group of Heathens who come together to worship, celebrate seasonal festivals, and create a supportive community.

Practices

Heathen rituals and practices are diverse, with variations between individual practitioners and different Heathen traditions. Blóts, or religious ceremonies, are commonly performed during solstices, equinoxes, and other key seasonal events to honor the gods and pay respects to the ancestors. These ceremonies often involve offerings, such as food, drink, or symbolic representations, which are given to the gods and then shared among the participants.

The use of altars, runes, and sacred symbols is also prevalent in Heathenry. Altars serve as a focal point for worship and often display representations or images of the gods, along with items of personal significance. Runes, the ancient alphabet of the Germanic peoples, hold both practical and mystical significance in Heathenry. They are used for divination, meditation, and creating magical intentions.

Norse Paganism and Honoring the Gods

Within the broader Heathenry movement, Norse Paganism holds a prominent position due to the rich mythology and historical sources available. Norse mythology, with its tales of gods, giants, heroes, and cosmic battles, provides a rich tapestry of stories and teachings. Many practitioners of Heathenry are drawn to the gods and goddesses of the Norse pantheon, as they are well-known figures with distinct personalities and attributes.

Honoring the gods in Norse Paganism often involves regular rituals, such as daily prayers or offerings. These acts of devotion can take various forms, including reciting poems or prayers, offering food and drink, or engaging in meditation and visualization. Some Heathens may choose to wear symbols or jewelry that represent their favored deities as a personal connection to their gods. The gods are seen as partners and guides, and their guidance is sought in matters of personal growth, practical matters, and spiritual endeavors.

Prevalence

The prevalence of Heathenry varies across different regions, with larger communities found in countries such as the United States, Canada, Germany, and the United Kingdom. Estimates of the number of Heathens worldwide are challenging to determine due to the decentralized and diverse nature of the belief system. However, it is believed that Heathenry has seen increased interest and growth in recent years as individuals explore alternative spiritual paths and seek connection with ancestral roots.

CHAPTER 5

The Wheel of the Year

I n this chapter, we delve into the captivating concept known as the
Wheel of the Year. This sacred wheel holds immense significance
for Pagans, as it connects them with the ever-changing rhythms of
nature and the profound energies associated with each season.

The Wheel of the Year represents the cyclic nature of life, death,
and rebirth that permeates everything in the Pagan worldview. It is
comprised of eight key festivals, or Sabbats, that mark the turning
points of the solar year. Each festival celebrates and honors specific
aspects of nature, celestial occurrences, and ancestral traditions.

The importance of the Wheel of the Year to Pagans lies in its ability
to deepen their spiritual connection to the earth and the divine
forces that inhabit it. Through the observance and participation
in these seasonal celebrations, Pagans align their energies with the
natural world, attuning themselves to the ebb and flow of the earth's
energy throughout the year.

Furthermore, the Wheel of the Year serves as a guide for personal
growth and self-reflection. Each festival offers an opportunity to
reflect on the lessons learned, set intentions, and welcome new
beginnings. As the wheel turns, Pagans embrace the concept of
continual renewal, mirroring the constant cycles found in nature.

Additionally, the Wheel of the Year fosters a sense of community
within Paganism. These festivals are often celebrated collectively,
bringing together individuals and groups united by a shared
reverence for the earth, spiritual harmony, and a deep connection to

ancient roots. The celebrations are marked by joyous rituals, feasts, music, dance, and merriment, enhancing the sense of inclusivity and togetherness.

Understanding the Pagan Calendar

The Pagan calendar, steeped in ancient lore and spirituality, offers a profound connection to the natural rhythms and cycles of the earth. It enables Pagans and those interested in nature-based spirituality to honor the seasons, celebrate the sacred and connect with the divine.

Paganism embraces a wide range of spiritual traditions, each with its distinct calendar. These calendars are often rooted in the ancient cultures and civilizations that revered nature and celebrated the changing seasons. Examples include the Celtic Wheel of the Year, the Wiccan Wheel, and the Norse calendar. While their names and details may vary, they all share a common purpose: to honor and align with the natural world.

We know that the Pagan calendar is commonly referred to as the Wheel of the Year, and it is divided into eight major festivals or Sabbats. These Sabbats mark the solstices, equinoxes, and points in between. By understanding these sacred points, Pagans can attune themselves to the energy of the season and tap into its power. Let's briefly explore the eight Sabbats and their significance:

- **Samhain (31st October):** Celebrated as the Pagan New Year, this festival marks the end of the harvest season and the beginning of the dark half of the year.

- **Yule/Winter Solstice (around 21st December):** The longest night, it represents the rebirth of the Sun and the return of light and hope.

- **Imbolc (1st February):** A time to honor the first signs of spring, Imbolc celebrates growth, purification, and the awakening of the earth.

- **Ostara/Spring Equinox (around 21st March):** The time of balance when day and night are of equal length, Ostara heralds the arrival of spring.

- **Beltane (1st May):** Also known as May Day, Beltane rejoices in the fertility and vitality of the earth as nature reaches its peak.

- **Litha/Summer Solstice (around 21st June):** The longest day of the year, Litha is dedicated to honoring the power of the Sun, abundance, and growth.

- **Lammas/Lughnasadh (1st August):** The first harvest festival, Lammas celebrates the ripening of crops and the gratitude for the earth's gifts.

- **Mabon/Autumn Equinox (around 21st September):** Signifying the arrival of autumn, Mabon emphasizes balance, reflection, and preparation for the darker months ahead.

To embrace the Pagan calendar and its wisdom, followers engage in various practices that connect them to nature and the cycles of life:

- **Observation:** Paying attention to the changes in the natural world, such as the blooming of flowers, falling of leaves, or the migration of birds, helps them attune to the seasons.

- **Rituals and celebrations:** Participating in ceremonies and rituals specific to each Sabbat allows Pagans to honor and express gratitude for the gifts and energy of that particular phase.

- **Deepening connection with nature:** Spending time outdoors, meditating, or incorporating elements like sacred herbs, crystals, or symbols associated with the Sabbat into daily practice can help strengthen the bond with nature.

- **Personal reflection:** Using the Pagan calendar as a guide, reflecting on personal journeys, and intentions can bring profound self-awareness and spiritual growth.

The Pagan calendar serves as a rich and meaningful guide for Pagans. By honoring and celebrating the changing seasons through rituals, ceremonies, and personal reflection, they deepen their connection to the earth and the divine forces that underpin all of existence.

Sabbats and Esbats: Celebrations and Rituals Throughout the Year

From the joyous celebrations of Beltane, where the air is filled with mirth and fertility, to the mystical and introspective Samhain, where the veil between the worlds is thin, each event is a unique celebration of nature, spirituality, and community. In this section, let's delve into each specific event and understand how it is celebrated in the Pagan community.

Samhain

Samhain is a significant festival celebrated by Pagans around the world. It falls on October 31st in the Northern Hemisphere and marks the end of the harvest season and the beginning of winter. The term Samhain, pronounced "sow-en" or "sow-in," originates from the Gaelic language and means "summer's end."

During Samhain, Pagans believe that the veil between the physical world and the spirit world is very thin. This is seen as a time when the ancestors and other supernatural beings can more easily interact with the living. Pagans hold great reverence for their ancestors and take the opportunity during Samhain to honor and remember them.

Pagans celebrate Samhain in various ways, some of which include:

• **Ancestor veneration:** Many Pagans create altars or shrines adorned with pictures and mementos of their deceased loved ones. They offer food, drink, and other items to honor and invite the spirits of their ancestors to join in the celebrations.

- **Rituals and ceremonies:** Rituals are performed to connect with the spirit world, seek guidance, and give thanks for the harvest. These can involve lighting bonfires, chanting, feasting, storytelling, and drumming. It is also a time for Pagans to reflect on personal growth and set intentions for the coming year.

- **Divination and fortune-telling:** As the veil thins, Pagans believe that this is an opportune time for divination and receiving messages from the spirit realm. Methods such as tarot card readings, scrying, and rune casting are commonly practiced to gain insights into the future.

- **Costuming and masquerading:** Samhain is traditionally seen as a time when the boundary between the living and the supernatural is blurred. Pagans often wear costumes, masks, or face paint to mimic spirits and confuse any malevolent entities that may be wandering between realms.

- **Community gatherings:** Pagans often come together as a community to celebrate Samhain. There might be public rituals in parks, community centers, or sacred sites, where people can share their traditions, stories, and experiences. This sense of connection and support is important to Pagans during this time.

Samhain is a time of reflection, remembrance, and renewal for Pagans. It invites individuals to acknowledge the cycles of life and death, honor the past, and embrace the coming darkness of winter with a sense of optimism and hope. It is a celebration that intertwines the sacred with the mundane, and Pagans treasure Samhain as an opportunity to deepen their spiritual connection and pay homage to their ancestors.

Yule

Yule is an enchanting celebration that has been observed by Pagans for centuries. It marks the winter solstice, the shortest day and longest night of the year, and is a time to embrace the return of light and the promise of new beginnings.

One of the most prominent symbols of Yule is the Yule log. Traditionally, a large log, often oak or pine, is carefully selected and brought into the home. It is then decorated with holly, evergreens, and ribbons before being placed in the fireplace or hearth. On the eve of Yule, the log is ceremoniously lit, symbolizing the return of the sun's light and warmth. As it burns, the embers are believed to carry blessings of good fortune for the coming year.

Candle lighting is another significant aspect of Yule celebrations. Many Pagans set up an Advent wreath or an altar adorned with candles representing the four elements: earth, air, fire, and water. Each week leading up to Yule, a new candle is lit, accompanied by prayers or intentions for the season. On the day of Yule itself, all the candles are lit together to honor the rebirth of the sun, illuminating the darkness of winter.

Feasting plays a vital role in Yule festivities. Pagans gather with loved ones to indulge in delicious, warming foods. Traditional dishes may include roasted meats, root vegetables, spiced drinks like mulled wine, and delectable desserts like gingerbread and Yule log-shaped cakes. Sharing a bountiful meal not only nourishes the body but also fosters a sense of community and gratitude for the abundance of the season.

Another cherished practice during Yule is gift-giving. Pagans exchange presents as a symbol of love, appreciation, and the giving of light. Many choose to create handmade gifts or offer items that hold personal significance, such as crystals, herbs, or sacred objects. These gifts are often accompanied by heartfelt messages or intentions, promoting connections, and fostering a deep sense of joy and generosity.

Additionally, connecting with nature is an integral part of Yule celebrations. Some Pagans participate in outdoor rituals, taking time to honor the winter landscape and its inhabitants. This can involve crafting bird feeders, leaving offerings for wildlife, or even going on a meditative stroll through a winter wonderland. By embracing the beauty of nature during this introspective time, Pagans strengthen their connection to the earth and all its cycles.

Imbolc

Imbolc, a traditional Pagan festival, is celebrated on February 1st or 2nd, marking the halfway point between the winter solstice and the spring equinox. It is a time to honor the return of the sun and the awakening of the earth, symbolizing the transition from darkness to light, from winter to the approaching spring.

In Pagan traditions, Imbolc is associated with the Celtic goddess Brigid, who represents healing, poetry, and smithcraft. Many rituals and celebrations are centered around her as well as themes of purification, renewal, and fertility. Here are some of the ways Pagans celebrate Imbolc:

- **Lighting of fires:** Fire plays a significant role in Imbolc celebrations, symbolizing the return of light and warmth. Fires are kindled to honor Brigid and to drive away winter's cold and darkness. Some practitioners light a large bonfire while others light candles or small hearth fires in their homes.

- **Brigid's crosses:** Brigid's crosses are woven from rushes, straw, or other pliable materials. They are placed above doorways or hearths to invoke the goddess's blessings and protection for the home. The crosses are also seen as symbols of the sun and are believed to bring good fortune and ward off evil.

- **Lighting candles:** Candles are lit to honor Brigid and to bring light and warmth into the home. Some people create altars with candles, flowers, and other symbols of spring. These altars serve as sacred spaces for meditation, reflection, and gratitude.

- **Blessing of seeds:** Imbolc is also a time to prepare for the upcoming planting season. Seeds are blessed and sometimes planted or placed on the altar. This ritual serves as a way to honor the cycles of nature and to invite abundance and growth.

- **Healing rituals:** As Brigid is associated with healing, this festival offers an opportunity to seek physical, emotional, and spiritual healing. Some Pagans may engage in rituals involving herbalism, meditation, energy work, or other forms of alternative healing.

- **Poetry and creative expression:** Brigid is also the goddess of poetry, inspiration, and creativity. Imbolc is a time for celebrating and honoring these gifts. Pagans may engage in activities like writing poetry, creating art, or even performing plays or music – all in reverence to the goddess.

It's important to mention that Imbolc celebrations vary among different Pagan communities and individuals. Some may choose to participate in public gatherings, while others prefer smaller, intimate rituals at home. Ultimately, the aim of these celebrations is to connect with the energy of the season, embrace the changing cycles of nature, and welcome the new beginnings that Imbolc brings.

Ostara

Ostara, also known as the Spring Equinox, is a joyous celebration of the changing season, new beginnings, and the arrival of spring. It is a time when day and night are of equal length, symbolizing balance, and harmony. Pagans and Wiccans honor this vibrant holiday by embracing the spirit of renewal, growth, and fertility.

One of the key traditions associated with Ostara is the decorating of eggs. These eggs are often beautifully painted or dyed in a myriad of colors, representing the blossoming of new life. The egg is seen as a potent symbol of fertility and rebirth. Some people even participate in egg rolling competitions, where they roll hard-boiled eggs down a hill, the winner being the egg that travels the farthest.

Another prominent aspect of Ostara is the focus on the natural world awakening from its winter slumber. Many Pagans celebrate by taking nature walks, observing the blooming flowers, budding trees, and the return of migratory birds. This serves as a way of reconnecting with the earth and appreciating the beauty and abundance it provides.

In addition, some Pagan communities organize bonfires or circle rituals to honor the rising sun and its strengthening powers. These gatherings often involve singing, dancing, storytelling, and the sharing of food. The bonfire acts as a beacon of warmth and light, symbolizing the growing strength and vitality of the sun as the days lengthen.

Planting seeds and tending to gardens is yet another tradition observed during Ostara. This act represents the nurturing of both physical and metaphorical seeds, encouraging personal growth and manifesting intentions for the coming months. People often start planting herbs, flowers, and vegetables during this time, as the earth's energy is believed to be most supportive of new beginnings.

Finally, it is common for Pagans to incorporate symbols of spring into their festivities. This includes adorning altars and homes with fresh flowers, sprigs of greenery, and representations of rabbits and hares, which are sacred creatures associated with fertility and abundance.

Beltane

Beltane, a joyous holiday celebrated by many Pagan traditions, marks the arrival of the vibrant spring season and the blossoming of life. It is a time of fertility, love, and growth, often observed on May 1st in the Northern Hemisphere.

The centerpiece of Beltane celebrations is the lighting of bonfires, symbolizing the return of warmth and light after the long, cold winter. Communities gather around these sacred fires, which are believed to ward off negative energies, bring prosperity, and kindle the energies of transformation. People dance and leap over the flames, invoking blessings and purification for the upcoming season.

Maypoles are another iconic feature of Beltane festivities. These tall, decorated poles represent the union of the masculine and feminine energies within nature. Colorful ribbons are tied to the top, and as participants joyfully dance and weave around the maypole, the ribbons intertwine to create a beautiful pattern. This ritual symbolizes the harmonious interplay of life's energies and is a celebration of love, fertility, and community.

Flowers and greenery play a significant role during Beltane. Garlands of fresh flowers are worn, hung throughout homes, and adorning altars. The influx of blooming plants and blossoms reflects the earth's vitality and abundance, reminding us of the richness and beauty of the natural world. Some Pagans also engage in the tradition of "Maying," where they awake before dawn to gather flowers and green branches, which are then brought into homes as a symbol of good luck.

Handfasting, a sacred ritual of commitment and love, is often consummated on Beltane. Couples bind their hands together with ribbons or cords, symbolizing their union and pledging to support and love each other. These ceremonies can range from private, intimate affairs to community celebrations, depending on personal preference. Many believe that Beltane is an auspicious time for weddings and commitment ceremonies due to its association with fertility and new beginnings.

Feasting and merriment are also integral to Beltane celebrations. Traditional foods like honeycakes, fresh fruits, and dairy products are enjoyed, celebrating the abundance of the season. Communities often come together for large feasts and communal picnics, fostering a sense of camaraderie and unity.

The spirit of Beltane is one of joy, playfulness, and gratitude. It is a time to awaken to the natural rhythms of the earth, to honor the growing life around us, and to celebrate the blessings of love and connection. Whether you choose to participate in one or all of these traditions, Beltane offers a perfect opportunity to embrace the renewal of life and partake in the rich tapestry of Pagan celebrations.

Litha

Litha, also known as Midsummer or the Summer Solstice, is a joyous and radiant celebration among Pagans. This sacred day, typically falling around June 20th-22nd, marks the longest day and the shortest night of the year. Pagans believe that the sun is at its peak power during Litha, symbolizing the triumph of light over darkness.

To celebrate Litha, Pagans engage in various traditions and festivities. One common practice is to gather in nature, particularly in areas such as fields, meadows, or near bodies of water. These natural settings help participants connect with the vibrant energy of the season. Bonfires are often lit as a representation of the sun's power, and people dance and leap through the flames for purification, protection, and to bring good fortune.

Flowers play a significant role during Litha as well. Many Pagans weave beautiful flower crowns or garlands to wear during the celebrations, symbolizing the abundance and fertility of the earth at its peak. These floral decorations are often placed on altars or hung as offerings to deities associated with growth and prosperity.

In addition to flowers, herbs are also highly revered during Litha. Many Pagans gather medicinal and magical herbs during this time, as it is said they possess potent healing and protective properties. Some even organize herbal workshops or create delicious herbal brews to share with others during the festivities.

As Litha is a celebration of the sun's energy, outdoor activities are popular among Pagans on this day. Special rituals may include activities like sun salutations, where individuals perform yoga or other movements to honor the sun's strength and vitality. Others may engage in traditional folk dances, singing songs, or playing music together in a harmonious celebration of life and nature.

Feasting is another integral part of Litha celebrations. Pagans often prepare and share meals with friends and family, enjoying seasonal fruits, vegetables, and grains. Some traditional dishes include ripe berries, fresh greens, lavish salads, and wheat-based breads. The meal becomes a collective expression of gratitude for the earth's bountiful gifts and the nourishment it provides.

As the sun finally sets on Litha, Pagans express gratitude for the abundance and light they have received. The rituals and celebrations during this time allow them to connect with nature's cycles, celebrating the beauty and fertility of the summer season.

Lammas

Lammas, also known as Lughnasadh, is a special Pagan holiday celebrated on August 1st or around that time each year. It marks the first harvest and the transition from summer to autumn. Pagans celebrate Lammas to honor the abundance and fertility of the earth, and to give thanks for the bountiful harvest that sustains us.

One common tradition during Lammas is the baking of bread using the new grains harvested. Pagans often gather together and bake bread as a symbol of gratitude for the earth's generosity. This act not only incorporates the sacredness of the harvest, but also represents the cycle of life, from the planting of seeds to the reaping of the harvest.

Another tradition during Lammas involves creating hand-woven corn dolls. These dolls, made from the husks of corn, represent the Harvest Mother or the corn goddess. They are often decorated with colorful ribbons and dried herbs and are placed on the altar or hung in the home to bring blessings and abundance.

Lammas is also a time for feasting and sharing the first fruits of the harvest. Pagan communities often come together to share a celebratory meal, where everyone brings food to contribute. The meal is a symbol of community, unity, and the interconnectedness of individuals with the land and each other.

Additionally, some Pagans choose to go on a nature walk or participate in outdoor activities during Lammas. They may gather in a nearby field or park, connect with nature, and honor the changing seasons. This can include activities like picking wildflowers, sharing stories and songs, or simply enjoying the beauty and abundance of the natural world.

Mabon

Mabon, also known as the Autumn Equinox, is a special time of year celebrated by Pagans to mark the transition from summer to fall. It is typically observed on or around September 21st in the Northern Hemisphere, and March 21st in the Southern Hemisphere. This festival holds significance for Pagans as it represents the balance between light and darkness, symbolizing the equal length of day and night.

During Mabon, Pagans gather to honor the harvest season and express gratitude for the abundance of nature. Here are a few traditions and practices specific to this festival:

- **Harvest feasts:** One of the central aspects of Mabon celebrations is the gathering of friends and family for a sumptuous feast. This meal often includes foods that represent the harvest, such as apples, pumpkins, squash, and root vegetables. Sharing food and coming together to enjoy a communal meal is a way to celebrate the bountiful gifts of the earth.

- **Crafting cornucopias:** The cornucopia, also known as the Horn of Plenty, is a symbol of abundance and prosperity. During Mabon, many Pagans create their own cornucopias as a craft project. These receptacles are then filled with dried leaves, nuts, and other natural items representing the autumnal season. It serves as a beautiful centerpiece and a reminder of the earth's generosity.

- **Making apple cider:** Apples are synonymous with fall, and making apple cider is a cherished tradition during Mabon. Pagans often gather apples from local orchards or their own gardens to press and create fresh cider. This process is a way to reconnect with the cycles of nature and appreciate the fruits of the season.

- **Nature walks and leaf collecting:** As the leaves begin to change colors, Mabon provides a wonderful opportunity for Pagans to take leisurely walks in nature. Collecting fallen leaves, acorns, and other natural treasures becomes an enjoyable and meditative activity. These collected items can later be used for crafts or altar decorations.

- **Rituals and gratitude ceremonies:** Mabon is a time to express gratitude for the blessings received throughout the year. Many Pagans perform rituals and ceremonies to acknowledge the balance between light and dark, giving thanks for what has been harvested and reflecting on the lessons learned. These rituals often involve lighting candles, offering prayers, and using herbs and flowers that embody the essence of autumn.

Remember, there are different types of Paganism and slightly different ways of celebrating each important festival across the Wheel of the Year.

CHAPTER 6

Connecting With Deities

While many religions emphasize the concept of a singular divine entity, Paganism embraces polytheism, acknowledging a pantheon of gods and goddesses. These deities manifest in various forms, each possessing unique qualities, attributes, and domains. From the wild and untamed gods of nature to the gentle and nurturing goddesses of love and empathy, Paganism offers a kaleidoscope of deities to connect with and seek guidance from.

Connecting with deities in Paganism is not merely a passive act of worship, but an active and personal relationship nurtured through ritual, meditation, and heartfelt devotion. In this chapter, we will explore both traditional and contemporary approaches to encountering and communing with these divine entities. Through these practices, Pagans seek to deepen their spiritual connection, enhance their understanding of self, and forge a profound bond with the gods and goddesses that resonate with their soul.

Building Relationships with Gods and Goddesses

Connecting with gods and goddesses in Paganism is a deeply personal and spiritual practice that can encompass a wide range of beliefs and traditions. While there are countless gods and goddesses worshipped in different Pagan traditions, this section aims to highlight some of the most important ones, provide guidance on how to connect with them, discuss the reasons behind this practice, and offer some important points to consider.

One of the fundamental principles of Paganism is the belief in a multitude of gods and goddesses, each representing different aspects of nature, life, and spirituality. These deities are often associated with specific elements, seasons, or natural phenomena, and are believed to have unique traits and powers that can be called upon for guidance, protection, and assistance. It's important to note that the gods and goddesses in Paganism are seen as distinct entities, rather than different aspects of a single higher being.

In Paganism, there is no one-size-fits-all approach to connecting with gods and goddesses, as practices vary greatly depending on individual beliefs and traditions. However, some common methods include prayer, meditation, ritualistic worship, offerings, and spiritual journeys. The specific methods used to connect with these deities often involve creating a sacred space, such as an altar or shrine, where individuals can focus their intentions and offer their devotion. Regular practice and the establishment of a personal relationship with the deities are key to strengthening this connection.

Why do Pagans seek to connect with gods and goddesses? The reasons are manifold and are shaped by the individual's spiritual journey and goals. Some seek guidance and wisdom from specific deities to navigate life's challenges, while others aim to foster a deeper connection with nature and the divine forces that permeate the world. Connecting with gods and goddesses can also be a form of expressing gratitude, reverence, and respect for their presence in one's life. Additionally, engaging in these practices can cultivate a sense of community and belonging within a wider Pagan community.

While each individual's path is unique, there are important points to consider when seeking to connect with gods and goddesses. First and foremost, it is essential to approach this practice with respect and an open mind. By recognizing the divine nature of these beings and showing reverence, individuals can establish a genuine connection based on mutual trust and understanding. However, it's crucial to remember that gods and goddesses in Paganism are not always benign or entirely predictable. They possess their own personalities, motivations, and agendas, and it is important to accept this and approach them with caution.

It's also important to acknowledge that not all deities are appropriate for everyone to work with. Just as in any relationship, compatibility plays a significant role. Take the time to research the attributes and characteristics of specific gods and goddesses to find those that resonate with your spiritual goals and values. Trust your intuition and inner guidance while discerning which deities you connect with most strongly.

Furthermore, an important aspect of connecting with gods and goddesses is to avoid cultural appropriation. It is essential to approach the practices and beliefs of different cultures with respect, and to honor the traditions and customs associated with specific deities. Learning about the cultural context in which a deity originated, understanding their stories and mythology, and seeking permission (if appropriate) can help ensure that the connection formed is genuine and authentic rather than appropriative.

Invocations, Prayers, and Offerings

Invocations, prayers, and offerings play important roles when interacting with deities in Paganism. These act as ways to establish a connection, express reverence, seek guidance, and show appreciation.

Invocations

Invocations are ritualistic calls to invite the presence and assistance of deities. They are often recited to establish a connection and to honor the specific qualities or aspects associated with the deity. Invocations can be personal and spontaneous, or they can be pre-written and used in group rituals. The intention behind an invocation is to create a sacred space and to invite the deity's energy and wisdom into that space.

When performing an invocation, it is important to approach the practice with sincerity and respect. Pagans begin by centering themselves and focusing on the presence of the deity they wish to invoke. They may choose to light candles, burn incense, or create a sacred altar to set the atmosphere. They speak clearly and with intention, addressing the deity by name and expressing their desire for their presence. They may also offer words of praise, acknowledging the deity's qualities and expressing their gratitude for their guidance and blessings. It's vital to speak from the heart and allow the energy of the invocation to flow.

Prayers

Prayers, on the other hand, are personal conversations with deities that can be done in various ways. They can take the form of spoken words, written letters, or even silent thoughts. Prayers are an opportunity for Pagans to express their deepest desires, share their hopes and fears, seek guidance, or simply offer gratitude. They are a means of communication and establishing a personal relationship with the divine.

To pray effectively, it is important to approach with clarity and focus. Pagans should find a quiet and comfortable space where they can concentrate without interruption. They may choose to light a candle or burn incense to create a sacred ambiance. They begin by centering themselves through deep breathing or meditation. Then, they speak or write their prayer, addressing the deity by name and expressing their intentions or requests.

It's important to be honest, sincere, and concise in this communication. After expressing a prayer, Pagans take a moment to be silent and listen for any messages or guidance that may come to them.

Offerings

Offerings are symbolic gifts given to deities as a way to express gratitude, seek blessings, and foster a reciprocal relationship. They can take the form of physical items, such as food, flowers, or personal belongings, or they can be intangible offerings, such as acts of service or devotion. Offerings can be made during rituals, ceremonies, or on specific occasions, such as festivals or holy days.

When making offerings, it is important to consider the preferences and cultural associations of the deity being honoring. It's vital to research the traditions and mythology associated with the specific deity to gain insight into appropriate offerings. For instance, if a Pagan is working with a lunar goddess, offering moon-shaped cakes or silver jewelry may be appropriate. Offerings should always be approach with respect and gratitude. Items can be placed on an altar or in a designated sacred space, and words can be spoken or expressed silently to communicate intentions and gratitude for the deity's presence. Ultimately, it is the thought and intention behind the offering that is most important.

While invocations, prayers, and offerings are essential practices in Paganism, it is important to follow some guidelines on what not to do. Firstly, Pagans should avoid making insincere or empty gestures. These practices should be approached with respect, commitment, and authenticity.

Pagans always research and understand the cultural traditions associated with the deities they are working with, and they take care to avoid appropriating practices without proper understanding and respect. Of course, promises or requests that are unrealistic or unethical should be avoided. It is crucial to approach deity interactions with integrity and to be aware of responsibilities and limitations.

Finding Your Patron Deity or Deities

In Paganism, a patron deity is a specific deity or god/goddess that an individual or group feels a strong connection with and chooses to honor and work with in their spiritual practice. Different Pagan traditions have different beliefs and practices, so the idea of a patron deity can vary.

Some Pagans may choose a patron deity based on their personal affinity or interests, while others may have a deity that reveals themselves through signs, dreams, or rituals. The relationship with a patron deity can be deeply personal, and individuals often work with their patron deity for guidance, connection, and spiritual growth.

Finding your patron or deity in Paganism is a deeply personal and unique journey, as there are countless gods and goddesses from different pantheons and mythologies to choose from. This process involves self-reflection, research, and a willingness to explore the realms of spirituality.

To begin this journey, Pagans first engage in self-reflection. They take some time to ponder their hopes, dreams, fears, and desires. Then, they consider the aspects of life that deeply resonate with them—the arts, wisdom, love, nature, healing, or perhaps something entirely different. Identifying these key aspects provide them with a starting point when searching for a patron or deity aligned with their personal values and interests.

Next, Pagans immerse themselves in the vast wealth of knowledge available about different mythologies and pantheons. There are numerous books, websites, and online communities dedicated to the study of mythology and Paganism. Experts and fellow practitioners can provide valuable insights into the characteristics and attributes of various deities.

When exploring different pantheons, it's vital to pay attention to how each culture worships their gods and goddesses. Do they engage in rituals, prayers, or offerings? Do they have specific symbols or sacred objects associated with each deity? Understanding how a particular culture approaches their deities can provide guidance on how to forge a meaningful connection with a chosen patron or deity.

Another fruitful avenue for discovering a patron or deity is through meditative practices. Pagans meditate on different qualities or aspects that resonate with them, and this can open the doors of perception and allow for a direct experience of a deity's presence. Through this, it's vital to be open and receptive to any messages or visions that may arise during these meditative journeys. These experiences can provide profound insights into the nature and purpose of the deity that may be calling out.

Additionally, divination methods such as tarot cards, runes, or pendulums can be used as tools for guidance. These practices can be used to pose questions to deities, and the answers can be interpreted through these divinatory techniques. Intuition is vital in this process.

Once Pagans find a patron or deity that resonates with them, it is essential to establish a connection and build a relationship through regular offerings, prayers, or rituals. These acts not only honor the deity but also deepen the bond between the follower and the deity.

CHAPTER 7

Sacred Spaces

Within Paganism, sacred spaces play an integral role as conduits of connection, where the boundaries between the physical and spiritual realms blur. These hallowed grounds are not only places of worship but also enclaves of healing, contemplation, and celebration.

At the heart of Paganism's relationship with sacred spaces lies the profound understanding of the interconnectedness of all living beings and the earth itself. Whether they take the form of ancient stone circles, secluded forests, mystical groves, or hidden rivers, these spaces—considered sacred by Pagans throughout the ages—hold immense power and resonance.

In Paganism, sacred spaces are revered for their ability to facilitate direct communion with deity, ancestors, and spirits of nature. Within these spaces, the veil between the mortal and divine realms becomes thinner, allowing prayers to be heard, spells to be cast, and rituals to be performed with profound intent.

Equally significant are the transformative qualities that these spaces possess. Stepping into them evokes a sense of awe and wonder, transcending the ordinary and opening doors to spiritual growth and personal exploration. They become portals, empowering practitioners to reconnect with their own inner divinity and seek wisdom and guidance from the natural world.

Moreover, sacred spaces provide sanctuary and solace for Pagans, serving as a sanctuary where they can let go of everyday concerns, find solace, and recharge their energies. It is within these spaces that they can be fully immersed in the embrace of nature, finding comfort and spiritual nourishment amidst the chaos of the modern world.

Creating Altars and Shrines

Altars and shrines hold deep significance in the practice of Paganism. They serve as sacred spaces for spiritual connection, devotion, and rituals.

An altar in Paganism is a physical space dedicated to honoring deities, ancestors, spirits, or sacred elements. It serves as a focal point for ritual practices, offering a tangible connection between the physical and spiritual realms. Altars can be found indoors, in private spaces, or outdoors amidst nature, depending on personal preference and tradition.

The construction and decoration of an altar in Paganism can vary greatly. Some followers prefer simplicity, while others embrace more elaborate designs. The key elements of an altar often include representations of the four cardinal elements—earth, air, fire, and water. These may be represented through corresponding tools such as stones, feathers, candles, or bowls of water. Additionally, altars often incorporate symbols of the deities or spirits being honored, such as statues, pictures, or symbols. These representations serve as focal points for devotion and meditation.

While altars are personal spaces, they are not limited to the individual. Many Pagan communities have shared altars that are utilized for group rituals, gatherings, or special events. These communal altars foster a sense of unity and collective spiritual experience.

Shrines, on the other hand, are distinct spaces dedicated to the veneration of specific deities, ancestors, or spirits. They can exist as standalone structures or can be integrated within an altar. Shrines often include unique offerings, such as specific foods, flowers, or objects associated with the entity being honored. They act as a space where prayers, petitions, and gratitude can be expressed in a focused manner.

The meaning and purpose of an altar or shrine vary based on individual beliefs and practices within Paganism. They function as spaces to engage in rituals, spellcasting, meditation, divination, and other spiritual practices. Altars and shrines facilitate communication with the celestial realms and allow for the building of relationships with higher powers.

Creating an altar or shrine is a highly personal and creative process. It begins by selecting the location and gathering the necessary items. Many Pagans choose a space that offers privacy, tranquility, and a connection to nature. Altars can be set up on a table, shelf, or any stable surface, while shrines may require more dedicated space or even a separate room.

Once the location is chosen, practitioners begin by laying a clean cloth as a foundation. This symbolizes the purity and sacredness of the space. Next, the elements and representations associated with the deities, spirits, or sacred entities are placed strategically on the altar. These items are often carefully chosen based on personal connections and correspondences. Candles, incense, crystals, and plants are popular choices, but the possibilities are endless.

Pagans engage with their altars and shrines in numerous ways. Offerings are a common practice, allowing practitioners to express gratitude, establish connections, and seek blessings. These offerings can range from small, symbolic objects to food, drink, or even personal items. Regular maintenance, such as cleaning and replenishing offerings, ensures the continued spiritual efficacy of the altar or shrine.

Rituals and ceremonies are an integral part of Pagan practice and often take place at altars and shrines. Rituals may involve prayers, chants, invocations, and the use of tools such as athames (ritual knives), wands, or cauldrons. These ceremonies serve to celebrate seasonal changes, honor deities, commemorate important life events, or seek guidance and protection.

Meditation is another vital aspect of Pagan practice, and altars and shrines provide an ideal space for this practice. Through meditation, practitioners can focus their energy, connect with higher powers, and explore the depths of their own spirituality. The serene environment of an altar or shrine facilitates a peaceful and introspective state of mind.

Outdoor Rituals and Working with Natural Elements

Key to Paganism is the practice of outdoor rituals and the incorporation of natural elements. These rituals serve as a means for Pagans to connect deeply with the earth, honor the cycles of nature, and cultivate a profound sense of interconnectedness.

Outdoor rituals are central to Pagan spiritual expression, serving as a way to establish a sacred space where practitioners can connect with both the physical and spiritual realms. Pagans recognize the inherent divinity found in nature and seek to harmonize with it through ritualistic practices.

These rituals often take place in serene natural settings such as forests, meadows, mountains, or near bodies of water. The chosen location is seen as a gateway to the divine, where the practitioner can draw upon the energy of the land.

Let's talk more about working with the elements and what each element means.

Earth, representing stability and grounding, is often associated with the physical realm and material abundance. Pagans may work with the element of Earth by incorporating herbs, plants, stones, or soil into their rituals or creating sacred altars adorned with natural objects. Working with Earth can provide a sense of security, bringing us closer to the natural cycles of growth and grounding us in the present moment.

Air, embodying communication, and intellect, is connected to thoughts, knowledge, and the power of the mind. Pagans may work with the element of Air through focused breathing exercises, meditation, or incorporating feathers or incense into rituals. Engaging with Air can help stimulate mental clarity, inspire creativity, and facilitate effective communication with both the self and others.

Fire, representing passion and transformation, symbolizes energy and action. Pagans may work with Fire by lighting candles, creating bonfires, or using fiery colors and symbols in their rituals. Fire is often seen as a catalyst for change and renewal, and working with this element can ignite motivation, willpower, and courage to pursue personal growth and transformation.

Water, representing emotions and intuition, is associated with the fluidity of life and the realm of the subconscious. Pagans may work with the element of Water by incorporating seashells, bowls of water, or natural bodies of water into their practices. Water helps us tap into our inner wisdom, connect with our emotions, and navigate the ebb and flow of life with greater ease.

Pagans understand that these elements are not only external forces but also inherent qualities within ourselves. By working with the elements, pagans seek to harmonize their own energies with the natural world, fostering a balanced and interconnected relationship.

Ultimately, the use of the elements in Paganism varies among individuals and traditions. Some may incorporate all four elements simultaneously in rituals or spell work, while others may focus on specific elements, depending on the intent or purpose of their practice. Regardless of the approach, the elements provide pagans with a powerful framework through which to attune with nature, celebrate the cycles of life, and deepen their spiritual connection.

The Significance of Sacred Sites in Paganism

Sacred sites hold immense significance in Paganism, acting as powerful portals that bridge the earthly realm with the divine. These sites exhibit a symbiotic relationship with nature, carrying the echoes of ancient rituals, mythology, and spiritual practices. From ancient stone circles to enchanted groves and natural landscapes, the allure of these places lies in their unique ability to evoke a deep spiritual experience.

Let's take a look at some of the most important sacred sites across the world.

Stonehenge

One of the most iconic and mysterious sacred sites in the world, Stonehenge, occupies a special place in Paganism. Located in England, this prehistoric monument captivates minds and hearts alike. The precise alignment of the stones with astronomical events, such as the solstices, has led to a deep belief in the site's connection with cosmic energies.

Pagans often gather at Stonehenge, particularly during the summer solstice, to celebrate the turning of the wheel of the year and to honor their ancestors' wisdom that resonates through time.

Avebury

Situated not far from Stonehenge, Avebury is another exceptional megalithic site that enchants Pagans. Avebury boasts the largest stone circle in Europe, encompassing the heart of a small village. Its energy is palpable, drawing visitors into a spiraling dance with the stones.

As a place of pilgrimage, Avebury holds great spiritual significance for those who seek to deepen their connections to the ancient past and the natural world.

Glastonbury Tor

Perched atop a hill in Somerset, England, Glastonbury Tor is a place of myth and legend. With its ancient tower visible for miles, the Tor has captured the imagination of countless Pagan pilgrims. It is believed to be the mythical Avalon, the place where King Arthur is said to have received Excalibur and where the mystical Isle of Apples resides.

Pagans journey to Glastonbury Tor to tap into the archetypal energy of magic and rebirth, commemorating the cycles of life.

Delphi

In ancient Greece, Delphi was revered as the center of the world and the home of the oracle. A sacred site dedicated to the god Apollo, Delphi was believed to act as a conduit between mortals and the divine. Pilgrims would travel great distances seeking wisdom and guidance from the oracle.

For modern Pagans, Delphi serves as a touchstone for connecting with the wisdom of the ancient gods, the power and mystery of divination, and the intrinsic connection between humanity and the divine.

Mount Shasta

Located in Northern California, Mount Shasta is a majestic peak shrouded in mystery and spiritual significance. It is widely regarded as a power spot, attracting many Pagan practitioners seeking spiritual renewal and personal transformation.

Believed to be one of Earth's energy vortexes, Mount Shasta is associated with various myths, including being the home of the hidden city of Telos, inhabited by an ancient race known as Lemurians. Its snowy slopes, pristine forests, and sparkling lakes provide the perfect backdrop for those seeking a spiritual retreat.

Sacred sites in Paganism represent a fusion of myth, history, and spiritual essence, beckoning individuals to continue their spiritual journeys, honor the land, and discover their own divine potential.

CHAPTER 8

Ethics and Morality in Paganism

Honoring the sacred cycles of nature, Paganism emphasizes the importance of living in harmony with the earth. As we embrace this ethos, we are called to be mindful custodians of the planet, recognizing that our choices and actions have far-reaching consequences. We are reminded to treat the natural world with reverence and gratitude, understanding that it is a source of infinite wisdom and nurturing energy.

Additionally, Paganism holds a deep reverence for life, celebrating its diversity and the inherent worth of every being. Through this lens, we are prompted to extend kindness, compassion, and understanding to all living creatures. We are encouraged to cultivate empathy and to treat others with respect and fairness, embracing the inherent dignity that resides within each person.

Of course, Paganism reminds us of our interconnectedness with the universe. It encourages us to recognize that every thought, word, and action ripples out into the vast web of existence. Thus, the choices we make in our daily lives hold an immense power and can shape the world around us. Through this awareness, we are invited to choose love over fear, unity over division, and harmony over discord.

As we embark on this exploration of ethics and morality in Paganism, may we embrace the beauty and wisdom this spiritual path has to offer. Let us discover how these guiding principles can enrich our lives, strengthen our bonds with others, and inspire us to become custodians of a more harmonious world.

The Wiccan Rede and the Threefold Law

The Wiccan Rede and the Threefold Law are both fundamental principles in Wiccan philosophy, guiding practitioners in their approach to magic, ethics, and personal responsibility. Understanding and embodying these principles is crucial for both beginners and experienced Wiccans alike.

The Wiccan Rede is a moral code that serves as a guiding principle for Wiccans. It can be summarized as "An it harm none, do what ye will." At its core, the Rede emphasizes the importance of non-harming and ethical behavior in all actions. It encourages individuals to consider the consequences of their choices on themselves and others before engaging in any action, ensuring that no harm is caused to the self or any other living being.

The term "Rede" originates from the Middle English word "rede," which means advice or counsel. The Wiccan Rede can be seen as the advice of wise Wiccan elders to abide by ethical principles when engaging in magic and pursuing their desires. It provides a framework for Wiccans to approach life with mindfulness and empathy.

The Wiccan Rede also acknowledges the freedom of personal will, highlighting the individuals' right to make choices that align with their true selves. However, this freedom is not to be taken as a license to harm others or act solely in self-interest. Wiccans strive to make decisions that are in harmony with the natural world and promote well-being for themselves and others.

The practical application of the Wiccan Rede can be seen in the ethical considerations that Wiccans take when working with magic. Before casting spells or engaging in any magical practice, they carefully consider the potential consequences. Wiccans believe that any energy they put out into the world, whether positive or negative, will return to them threefold. This brings us to the Threefold Law.

The Threefold Law is a principle closely tied to the Wiccan Rede that states, "Whatever energy or action is put into the world, whether positive or negative, will be returned to the sender three times over." This principle reflects the belief in karma, asserting that the consequences of our actions reverberate back to us with three times the intensity. It serves as a powerful reminder that our choices and intentions have weight and resonance in the universe.

Understanding the Threefold Law helps Wiccans cultivate mindfulness, accountability, and responsibility in their actions. It guides them to strive for harmony, empathy, and positive intentions to ensure that the energy they send out into the universe yields positive outcomes in their lives as well.

The Threefold Law should not be mistaken as a simplistic system of rewards and punishments. It is not about moral judgment or retribution. Instead, it is a spiritual concept that encourages individuals to become aware of the interconnectedness of all beings and the impact they have on the world around them. By practicing empathy and mindfulness, Wiccans seek to create a positive ripple effect that benefits themselves, others, and the natural world.

The Wiccan Rede and the Threefold Law both emphasize the importance of personal responsibility and ethical consideration. They invite individuals to view their actions and choices through the lens of compassion, empathy, and holistic well-being. Through the application of these principles, Wiccans strive to live in harmony with nature, forge deeper connections with their spiritual selves, and create positive change in the world.

Concepts of Karma and Responsibility

Central to the Pagan belief system are the concepts of karma and responsibility, which guide Pagans on their journey toward self-awareness, personal growth, and ethical living.

Derived from ancient Eastern philosophies, the concept of karma finds resonance within Paganism, albeit with its unique interpretations. Unlike the popular misconception of karma as mere cause and effect, Pagans perceive it as a holistic cosmic law encompassing all aspects of life. Karma in Paganism emphasizes the intricate interplay between intention, action, and consequence, shaping an individual's spiritual evolution and influencing their interactions within the web of life.

According to Pagan belief, every action we undertake, whether positive or negative, creates an energetic ripple that reverberates throughout the universe. These energetic imprints, or karmic imprints, accumulate and influence not only our present circumstances but also our future experiences. This understanding of karma inspires Pagans to approach life with mindfulness, cultivating positive intentions and responsible actions that contribute to the collective well-being.

Responsibility to Self and Others

One of the core tenets of Paganism is the recognition of personal responsibility. Pagans trust that every individual possesses agency and the power to shape their own destiny through intentional actions. This responsibility extends beyond oneself to the wider community and the environment. Pagans see themselves as guardians of the earth, with the duty to protect and preserve its beauty and resources.

In this perspective, living responsibly means being in harmony with nature, respecting the diversity of life, and embracing sustainable practices. Pagans strive to minimize their ecological footprint, supporting ethical and sustainable choices in their daily lives. They emphasize a deep sense of connection to the natural world, understanding that harming the environment ultimately harms themselves and future generations.

Healing and Reconciliation

Within the framework of karma and responsibility, Pagans also acknowledge the potential for healing and reconciliation. Recognizing that we are fallible beings prone to making mistakes, Pagans emphasize the importance of acknowledging and learning from past actions. By taking responsibility for their deeds, individuals embark on a path of personal growth and self-transformation.

Pagans believe in the power of forgiveness, both for ourselves and for others. Through forgiveness, individuals release themselves from the burdens of guilt, resentment, and negative karmic imprints. By seeking reconciliation and understanding, they open the door to creating harmonious relationships and fostering a more compassionate and tolerant world.

Put simply, the concepts of karma and responsibility provide a moral compass for individuals seeking a deeper understanding of their place in the interconnected web of life. Responsibility in Paganism extends beyond us to encompass care for the earth and all its inhabitants, embracing sustainable practices and fostering a sense of harmony.

Respect for All Living Beings

In Paganism, the belief in respecting all living beings is deeply ingrained in its core principles. The interconnectedness of all life is central to this spiritual tradition, with Pagan practitioners recognizing the inherent worth and dignity of every living being. This respect extends not only to humans but also to animals, plants, and the entire natural world.

Paganism celebrates the diversity and uniqueness of life forms, acknowledging that every living being holds an important place in the intricate web of existence. From the smallest insect to the mightiest tree, each entity is seen as having its own purpose and wisdom to share. This reverence for all life stems from the understanding that all beings are interconnected and dependent on one another for survival and wellbeing.

One of the fundamental concepts underlying respect for all living beings in Paganism is the belief in animism. Animism is the idea that everything in the universe possesses a soul or a spirit. From rocks and rivers to animals and plants, everything is alive and deserving of respect. This perspective encourages Pagans to treat all living beings with kindness and consideration, honoring their intrinsic value and contribution to the greater whole.

Pagan rituals often involve offerings or acts of gratitude toward the natural world. Whether it be leaving food and water for wildlife, planting trees, or participating in ecological clean-up efforts, Pagans actively engage in practices that demonstrate their respect for the environment and its inhabitants. By recognizing the value of all life forms, Pagans strive to foster a harmonious relationship with nature, promoting balance and sustainability.

Moreover, Paganism holds deep respect for animals and views them as sacred counterparts to humans. Many Pagan traditions incorporate animal symbolism and totemism, where individuals identify with or have a special affinity for specific animals. These animals are seen as spiritual guides, providing insight and wisdom to those who are open to their messages. As such, Pagans greatly respect and appreciate the contributions that animals make to their lives and the natural world as a whole.

In Pagan ethical frameworks, the principle of compassion plays a significant role. By embodying compassion toward all living beings, Pagans aim to minimize harm and suffering in the world. This involves conscious efforts to consider the consequences of one's actions and make choices that prioritize the wellbeing of others. From the food they consume to the products they use, Pagans strive to align their lifestyle with their belief in respect for all life forms.

The concept of respect for all living beings extends beyond the physical realm in Paganism. Pagans also have a deep connection with the spiritual realms and believe in the existence of various deities, spirits, and ancestors. They recognize and honor these beings as valuable contributors to the overall tapestry of existence, showing them reverence and respect through offerings, prayers, and rituals.

Furthermore, Paganism encourages a sense of stewardship toward the earth and its resources. Many Pagans embrace eco-friendly practices such as recycling, composting, and reducing waste as a means to minimize their environmental impact. By doing so, they demonstrate their respect for the earth and actively work toward preserving its beauty and abundance for future generations.

CHAPTER 9

Magic and Spell Craft

M agic, an ancient and wondrous concept, has captivated human beings throughout history. From the ancient Egyptians to the Native Americans, people across cultures and continents have sought to harness the power of magic. In the realm of Paganism, magic holds a special place, serving as a way to connect with the natural world, tap into ancestral energies, and manifest one's desires.

At its core, magic in Paganism is the manipulation and channeling of natural energies in order to bring about change. This change can be both internal and external, affecting the individual practitioner or the surrounding environment. It is important to note, however, that magic within Paganism is not synonymous with the stage magic or illusions we often see in mainstream media. Rather, it is a deeply spiritual practice rooted in ancient beliefs and customs.

One key aspect of understanding magic in Paganism lies in the recognition of interconnectedness. Pagans believe that everything in the universe is connected through a web of energy, commonly referred to as the "web of Wyrd" or "web of life." This web connects not only all living beings but also the elements of nature, celestial bodies, and spiritual entities. The foundation of Pagan magic lies in the ability to tap into this web and manipulate its energies to create change.

Another fundamental principle of magic in Paganism is the belief in the existence of unseen spirits or deities that can be called upon for assistance and guidance. These spirits can range from nature spirits such as faeries or nymphs, to gods and goddesses associated with specific aspects of life and nature. In Pagan magic, practitioners often invoke these spiritual beings through rituals, prayers, and offerings to seek their aid in their magical workings.

The practice of magic in Paganism can take many forms and is often tailored to individual beliefs and traditions. Some Pagans may work with herbs, crystals, and natural objects to harness their energies, while others may focus on divination, spellcasting, or ritualistic ceremonies. Regardless of the method, the underlying principle remains the same: to align with the natural energies and forces of the universe in order to shape one's reality.

One of the most important aspects of magic in Paganism is the concept of personal responsibility and ethical considerations. Unlike the portrayal of magic in popular culture, Pagan magic emphasizes the ethical use of one's power. Practitioners are encouraged to follow a code of conduct that typically includes principles such as "do no harm," "act in alignment with nature," and "honor the interconnectedness of all beings." This ethical approach ensures that magic is used for the greater good and for the betterment of oneself and the world around them.

Understanding magic in Paganism also requires an understanding of the cycles of nature and the seasons. Pagans often align their magical workings with the changing tides of the natural world, using the energy of the solstices, equinoxes, and other significant celestial events. This connection to nature's cycles allows practitioners to tap into the seasonal energies and work in harmony with the ebb and flow of life.

Additionally, Pagan magic places great importance on rituals and ceremonies. These practices serve as a way to commune with the divine, to connect with ancestral energies, and to bring about a heightened state of consciousness. Rituals can involve elements such as meditation, chanting, drumming, dance, and the use of sacred tools. Through these practices, practitioners aim to create a sacred space where magic can thrive and manifest their intentions.

It is worth noting that the understanding of magic in Paganism is incredibly diverse and adaptable. Different Pagan traditions and individual practitioners may have their own unique beliefs and practices when it comes to magic. This flexibility allows for a rich and vibrant tapestry of magical customs and rituals within the Pagan community.

Types of Spells and Their Purposes

Spells hold a significant place in Paganism as powerful tools for manifesting desires, connecting with divine energies, and working with the forces of nature. These spells vary in nature, purpose, and intent, each serving a different facet of spiritual practice.

Protection Spells

Protection spells are a fundamental aspect of Paganism, aimed at safeguarding individuals, spaces, or objects from negative energies, harmful influences, or malicious intentions.

These spells often involve the creation of energetic barriers, invoking deities or spirits associated with protection, and harnessing natural elements such as herbs, crystals, or charms. From personal amulets to wards for homes, protection spells provide a sense of security and serenity in the face of adversity.

Healing Spells

Healing spells focus on restoring balance and well-being, addressing physical ailments, mental distress, emotional imbalances, or spiritual disconnection. These spells may incorporate the use of herbs, essential oils, crystals, visualization techniques, or energy manipulation to harness the body's innate healing capacities.

Whether it's a soothing spell for a troubled mind or a remedy for physical pain, healing spells foster holistic well-being, and promote self-care and inner growth.

Love and Relationship Spells

Love spells are rituals designed to attract, enhance, or foster love within oneself or between individuals. They aim to invoke the energies of love, passion, and harmony, encouraging deep connections and fostering healthy relationships.

Such spells might involve the use of candles, herbs, written intentions, or rituals imbued with particular incantations and symbols. It's important to approach love spells with ethics and respect for the free will of individuals involved, focusing on enhancing the love within oneself instead of manipulating others.

Prosperity Spells

Prosperity spells focus on nurturing abundance, prosperity, and financial well-being. These spells tap into the energies of abundance and gratitude, invoking cosmic forces to attract wealth, success, and opportunities. They may involve techniques such as affirmations, candle magic, sigils, or offering rituals to deities associated with abundance and prosperity.

It is essential to approach prosperity spells with the understanding that they work in alignment with our practical efforts and not as a substitute for hard work or responsible financial decision-making.

Divination Spells

Divination spells play a pivotal role in Pagan traditions, allowing practitioners to seek guidance, gain insight, and access hidden knowledge. From tarot card readings to scrying and rune casting, divinatory spells serve as a bridge between the material and spiritual realms.

By channeling energy, focusing intent, and utilizing various divination tools, these spells seek to unveil the mysteries of the universe, offering guidance, clarity, and a deeper understanding of one's path.

Cleansing and Purification Spells

Cleansing and purification spells are employed to rid oneself, spaces, or objects of negative energy, spiritual stagnation, or any lingering disharmony.

These spells often involve the use of smudging with sacred herbs such as sage or palo santo, sprinkling blessed water or salt, or performing rituals to release stagnant energy. They enable practitioners to create a harmonious and sacred environment, paving the way for spiritual growth, clarity, and positive energy flow.

Manifestation Spells

Manifestation spells are potent tools used to transform desires and intentions into tangible reality. By harnessing the power of focused intent, visualization, and energy manipulation, practitioners aim to align their energies with their desired outcomes. These spells may involve candle magic, creative visualization, or the use of specific symbols charged with intention. However, it's essential to remember that manifestation spells are most effective when aligned with one's highest good and do not infringe upon the free will of others.

Ethics of Spell Casting and Responsible Use of Magic

The concepts of respect, intention, and responsibility form the pillars upon which the ethics of spell casting and the responsible use of magic are built. In this section, we will delve into these key principles and explore how they guide practitioners in maintaining a harmonious balance between their magical endeavors and the world around them.

Respect for Nature and the Divine

Central to Paganism is the reverence for nature and the acknowledgment of the divine essence that permeates all living beings. In the ethics of spell casting, respecting these fundamental aspects is of utmost importance. As such, Pagan practitioners strive to align their magical workings with the natural rhythms and cycles of the earth. They understand that all actions have consequences and believe in the interconnectedness of all things.

When casting spells or performing magical rituals, ethical practitioners prioritize obtaining consent, not only from human participants but also from the natural world and the spiritual entities involved. This respect extends to using ethically sourced materials and environmentally friendly practices. By adhering to these principles, Pagan spellcasters strive to ensure that their magic is in harmony with nature and respects the divine essence within themselves and others.

Intention and the Law of Return

Another essential aspect of responsible spell casting is the consideration of intention and the Law of Return. The Law of Return, also known as the Threefold Law or Law of Karma, states that whatever energy or intent is put into the universe will return threefold to the individual who casts the spell.

This principle reminds practitioners of the profound impact their actions can have and encourages them to be mindful of their motivations and the potential consequences of their spells.

Ethical spellcasters understand the importance of aligning their intentions with positivity and the greater good. They avoid using magic to manipulate or harm others, recognizing that such actions can disrupt the balance and create negative energy within the universe. Instead, they focus on spells that promote healing, growth, love, and transformation.

By always taking into account their intentions and the potential repercussions, ethical practitioners remain conscious of their responsibilities as magical beings.

Responsible Use of Power

Knowing when and how to wield magical power responsibly is vital for any ethical spellcaster. Pagan practitioners understand that magic is a tool that should never be used for personal gain or to exert control over others. They recognize that true power lies in the ability to influence positive change within themselves and the world around them.

To ensure responsible use of magic, ethical practitioners engage in self-reflection and introspection, continuously evaluating their motives and the potential impact of their spells. By remaining humble and acknowledging their limitations, they prioritize the well-being of others, favoring spells that promote harmony and respect for the autonomy of individuals.

Education and Accountability

As with any practice, education is key to ethical spell casting and the responsible use of magic. Pagan practitioners are encouraged to continually expand their knowledge, understanding, and skill set in order to ensure the safe and effective use of spells. This includes studying the various magical traditions, history, and lore, as well as familiarizing themselves with the cultural and spiritual contexts in which their magic is practiced.

Accountability is another critical aspect within Pagan ethics. Practitioners are encouraged to take responsibility for their magical actions and their consequences. This includes acknowledging and learning from any mistakes made, as well as actively seeking to amend any harm caused. Ethical spellcasters strive to continuously develop their skills and understanding, building a strong foundation for the responsible use of magic.

CHAPTER 10

The Role of Community in Paganism

While beliefs and practices may differ among Pagan individuals, the sense of belonging to a community is a common thread that intertwines them all.

In Paganism, community provides a nurturing ground for individuals to connect with like-minded souls who share similar perspectives and spiritual aspirations. By joining together, Pagans find solace in knowing that they are not alone on their spiritual path, but rather surrounded by kindred spirits who offer guidance, wisdom, and companionship.

The power of community extends beyond individual growth; it becomes a source of inspiration and empowerment for collective rituals, celebrations, and communal efforts. Through shared ceremonies, festivals, and gatherings, Pagans nourish their connection to nature, deities, and each other, forging bonds that strengthen both their personal and collective identities.

Moreover, community serves as a catalyst for the exchange of knowledge, customs, and rituals, ensuring the continuity and preservation of Pagan traditions across generations. The passing down of wisdom, mentorship, and teachings within the Pagan community bolsters the richness and diversity of this path, creating a practice that honors the past while embracing the present.

Finding and Joining Pagan Communities

Embarking on a spiritual journey often involves seeking out like-minded individuals who share similar beliefs and values. For those interested in Paganism, connecting with supportive and nurturing communities can be an invaluable part of their path.

In this section, we will explore some practical steps to help you find and join Pagan communities that resonate with your spiritual aspirations.

Research and Exploration

The first step toward finding a Pagan community is researching different traditions and belief systems within Paganism. Familiarize yourself with various paths such as Wicca, Druidry, Heathenry, and Shamanism.

Read books, blogs, and websites that offer insights into these traditions, allowing you to understand their principles and practices. This research will help you define your own spiritual inclinations and establish a foundation for your journey toward finding the right community.

Online Communities and Forums

The internet has become a vibrant hub for Pagan communities. Engaging with online forums, message boards, and social media platforms dedicated to Paganism can help you connect with like-minded individuals from around the world.

Websites like Witchvox and The Cauldron offer forums and local events directories that can aid in finding Pagan gatherings, festivals, and covens in your area. Engage in conversations, ask questions, and share experiences to establish connections and gather valuable insights from seasoned practitioners.

Local Pagan Gatherings and Events

Attend local Pagan gatherings, events, and workshops in your area. Often organized around Sabbats and Esbats, these gatherings provide an excellent opportunity to meet other Pagans, explore different practices, and expand your knowledge.

Attend workshops, participate in rituals, and connect with organizers or attendees to discover welcoming communities nearby. Local metaphysical stores, pagan-friendly bookshops, and libraries may carry information about upcoming events.

Seek Out Nature-Based Groups

Paganism is often rooted in a deep reverence for nature and the cycles of the seasons. Connecting with nature-based groups can be an enriching experience for Pagan seekers. Join nature hikes, ecological projects, and environmental organizations with a spiritual focus.

These groups often attract Pagan individuals who share a similar spiritual connection to the natural world, providing an opportunity to meet potential community members who align with your beliefs.

Seek Guidance from Elders and Local Leaders

In your search for Pagan communities, it can be beneficial to reach out to local Pagan elders or leaders. Seek guidance and advice from individuals who have been practicing Paganism for years and have established connections within the community. Elders can often provide valuable insights, recommend appropriate groups, or even help you find a mentor to guide you as you navigate your spiritual journey.

Pagan Festivals and Gatherings

Pagan festivals and gatherings provide an immersive environment for engaging with a larger community. These events are an excellent opportunity to meet a wide range of practitioners, participate in rituals, attend workshops, and socialize with others sharing your spiritual path.

Events like PantheaCon, Beltane Fire Festival, or Pagan Spirit Gathering attract practitioners from near and far, allowing you to connect with diverse Pagan communities and find like-minded individuals.

Pagan Covens and Study Groups

If you are looking for a more intimate setting, consider joining a Pagan coven or study group. Covens are small, tightly knit communities that practice together, celebrate rituals, and nurture spiritual growth. Seek out covens or study groups that resonate with your beliefs and interests.

Attend open rituals or workshops hosted by covens to get a feel for their energy, philosophy, and compatibility with your own spiritual path.

Finding and joining Pagan communities is an essential aspect of the spiritual journey for many people interested in Paganism. Remember to approach this process with an open mind, be respectful of different paths, and trust your intuition to find a community that feels like a true spiritual home. Embrace the journey and enjoy the transformative experience of becoming part of a vibrant Pagan community.

Celebrating Special Occasions in Pagan Communities

Pagan communities across the world come together to honor and commemorate special occasions, such as solstices, equinoxes, holidays, and personal milestones. In this section, let's explore how Pagans celebrate these special occasions, shedding light on their unique rituals, traditions, and the sense of unity that arises within these vibrant communities.

Gatherings for the Wheel of the Year

A significant aspect of Pagan celebrations revolves around the Wheel of the Year, which comprises eight major holidays. These holidays mark significant points in nature's cycles, creating opportunities for Pagans to connect with the natural world and their spiritual beliefs.

For example, the solstices and equinoxes serve as pivotal moments of balance and transition, known as Sabbats. Pagans often gather in outdoor spaces, such as parks or sacred groves, to observe rituals that align with the changing seasons. These ceremonies involve various practices, including meditation, dancing, music, and the recitation of prayers or affirmations.

Additionally, Pagans celebrate the four fire festivals (Samhain, Imbolc, Beltane, and Lughnasadh) to mark the agricultural and seasonal changes throughout the year. These festivals light up the community with bonfires, feasts, and intricate rituals that symbolize the cycle of life, death, and rebirth.

Communal Customs and Rituals

Pagan celebrations are steeped in diverse customs and rituals that allow individuals to express their spirituality and foster a sense of camaraderie within their community.

One common tradition is the creation of a sacred circle, often laid with herbs, flowers, or crystals. This circle acts as a boundary between the everyday world and the sacred space where rituals take place. It represents protection and unity, symbolizing the equality of all participants.

An essential tool within Pagan celebrations is the ritual athame, a ceremonial knife used to direct energy during spells or invocations. During special occasions, Pagans often share their athames, allowing each individual to contribute to the collective energy and intention of the gathering.

In addition, chanting, singing, and drumming are central to Pagan rituals. These forms of sonic expression connect individuals more deeply with their spiritual selves and foster a collective energy that encapsulates the essence of the celebration.

Feasting and sharing meals hold great significance in Pagan celebrations. The community often comes together for potluck-style feasts, where everyone brings a dish to share. This act of nourishing the body and soul enhances the sense of unity and creates a space for deeper connections to form.

Rites of Passage and Personal Milestones

Pagan communities also come together to celebrate personal milestones and rites of passage in the lives of their members. These occasions, ranging from birthdays to handfasting ceremonies, allow Pagans to honor key moments and support one another through life's journeys.

Handfasting, the Pagan equivalent of a wedding ceremony, represents the commitment of two individuals to each other. These ceremonies are often held outdoors, with rituals that incorporate elements such as binding of hands with colorful cords, exchanging vows, and invoking blessings from the four elements.

Naming ceremonies, which celebrate the birth or adoption of a child, are also significant events in Pagan communities. These celebrations often involve the breaking of the child's connection to the spirit world, symbolizing their entrance into the earthly realm. Participants may offer gifts, blessings, or words of wisdom to the child and their parents.

Moreover, coming-of-age ceremonies are observed when young individuals reach a significant stage in their lives, signifying their transition from childhood to adulthood. These ceremonies often include mentorship and teachings from more experienced members of the community, enabling young Pagans to embrace their unique spiritual paths.

Supporting One Another on the Spiritual Path

In a world that often embraces conformity, those seeking alternative spiritual paths can find solace and support within Pagan communities. Pagans, with their varied belief systems and diverse practices, foster an environment that encourages personal growth, exploration, and understanding.

Let's explore the ways in which Pagans support one another along their spiritual paths.

Mentoring and Apprenticeship

Within Pagan communities, elders, and experienced practitioners often mentor those who are just beginning their spiritual journeys or seeking to deepen their practices. These mentors provide guidance, knowledge, and emotional support to those who seek it. Apprenticeship programs allow individuals to learn from seasoned practitioners, providing a structured path for personal growth.

Mentors can aid in the development of a strong spiritual foundation, helping individuals navigate their way through the vast and sometimes overwhelming world of Paganism. By sharing their own experiences, mentors empower their mentees to explore their unique path with confidence, while respecting the diversity and individuality of each seeker.

Networking and Resource Sharing

Pagan communities have embraced modern technology as a means to connect on a global scale, fostering vibrant networks of support. Online forums, social media groups, and specialized websites bring together Pagans from all walks of life. Through these platforms, individuals can seek advice, share knowledge, and find resources pertinent to their spiritual growth.

Digital spaces dedicated to Paganism facilitate discussions on various spiritual topics, allowing individuals to engage in meaningful dialogue and broaden their perspectives. Whether seeking information on herbs and crystals, divination techniques, or sharing personal stories and insights, networking within the Pagan community offers boundless opportunities for support and education.

Collective Advocacy and Activism

Pagans often join forces to advocate for religious freedom and to protect the rights of their communities. Through collective activism, they work to dispel misconceptions surrounding Paganism and promote acceptance and understanding. Whether through participating in interfaith dialogues, organizing public rituals, or advocating for policy changes, Pagans stand together to ensure their spiritual paths are legally and socially recognized.

By uniting their voices, Pagans work toward creating a world where people can freely express their spirituality without fear of discrimination or persecution. This collective advocacy strengthens the bonds within the community, empowering individuals to take ownership of their spiritual paths while supporting others to do the same.

Pagans understand that spirituality is a personal journey, but they also recognize the immense power of community and collective support. Through shared rituals, mentorship, networking, and collective advocacy, Pagans create an inclusive and empowering environment for individuals to explore and embrace their unique spiritual paths. The supportive nature of Pagan communities fosters personal growth, self-discovery, and an unyielding commitment to celebrating life in all its diverse and magical forms.

CHAPTER 11

Paganism in Modern Society

P aganism, with its ancient roots in various earth-centered
spiritual traditions, has found a place of relevance and
significance in the modern world. Despite the passing of centuries,
Paganism continues to resonate with many people seeking a
spiritual path that connects them with nature, honors their ancestral
heritage, and fosters a sense of community.

One of the reasons Paganism has endured and adapted to the modern
world is its inherent flexibility and inclusivity. Unlike organized
religions with strict dogmas, Paganism embraces a diverse range of
beliefs and practices. As a result, followers can incorporate elements
from various cultures, mythologies, and spiritual practices into
their personal paths, making it a truly unique and individualized
experience. This ability to mix and match allows Pagans to adapt
their practices to fit their present-day needs and values.

Paganism's connection to nature is another aspect that resonates
strongly in the modern world. With concerns about environmental
degradation and climate change, many individuals are seeking
spiritual paths that emphasize sustainable living and reverence
for nature. Paganism, with its focus on the cycles of the earth and
the interconnectedness of all living beings, provides a framework
for reconnecting with the natural world and developing a sense of
ecological responsibility.

Moreover, Paganism offers a space for those who feel disconnected
from mainstream religious traditions or who are seeking alternatives
to rigid hierarchical systems. With its emphasis on personal gnosis,

or direct spiritual experience, Paganism encourages individuals to explore their own unique relationship with the divine. This freedom allows for a more inclusive and egalitarian approach to spirituality, where everyone's voice and experiences are valued.

Paganism's ancient roots also add a sense of depth and wisdom to modern life. In a fast-paced world often focused on immediate gratification, many individuals are drawn to the wisdom of their ancestors and the timeless traditions of Paganism. Exploring the mythology, rituals, and folklore of ancient cultures can provide a sense of grounding and connection with the past, creating a bridge between ancient wisdom and the challenges of the present.

Challenges and Misconceptions

In the modern world, Paganism often finds itself facing numerous challenges and misconceptions. As an ancient and diverse spiritual path, Paganism encompasses a wide range of beliefs and practices that honor nature, ancestors, and interconnectedness. However, due to its rich history and the general lack of knowledge about Paganism, misconceptions and challenges arise.

This section aims to shed light on some of these challenges and misconceptions, while also offering insights and understanding for those seeking to embrace the path of Paganism.

Misconception: Equating Paganism with Satanism

One of the most pervasive misconceptions about Paganism is that it is synonymous with Satanism or devil worship. This misunderstanding is often fueled by the distorted portrayal of Paganism in popular media.

In reality, Paganism is a diverse and nature-centered spiritual path that respects the interconnectedness of all beings and holds reverence for deities associated with nature, not evil entities.

Educating others about the true essence of Paganism can help dispel this misconception.

Misconception: Lack of Morality or Ethics

Another misconception surrounding Paganism is the belief that its followers lack a moral compass or a structured ethical system. This misperception arises due to the absence of a central religious authority in Paganism.

However, Paganism, like any spiritual path, encompasses a diverse range of ethical principles and moral values. Many Pagan traditions emphasize the importance of personal responsibility, harm reduction, environmental stewardship, and respect for all life. Educating others that Paganism embraces a strong ethical framework can help challenge this misconception.

Misconception: Practicing Witchcraft as Inherently Evil

Witchcraft, an integral part of many Pagan traditions, is often misunderstood and portrayed negatively in society. This misconception stems from the historical persecution and demonization of witches, which still carries echoes in modern times.

Contrary to such misconceptions, witchcraft is a spiritual practice focused on harnessing natural energies, affirming personal power, and manifesting positive change. By providing accurate information about the multifaceted nature of witchcraft, Paganism can challenge this misconception and nurture a better understanding of its practices.

Challenge: Social Stigmatization and Prejudice

Due to the prevalence of misconceptions surrounding Paganism, followers often face social stigmatization and discrimination. Many Pagans choose to remain in the proverbial "broom closet" due to fear of judgment or persecution.

This challenge can lead to feelings of isolation and hinder an individual's personal or spiritual growth. Advocacy and education play a vital role in breaking down stigmas and fostering inclusivity. Open discussions, building bridges with other religious communities, and emphasizing common values can help overcome this challenge and promote acceptance.

Challenge: Lack of Representation and Safe Spaces

Paganism often struggles with visibility in mainstream society, with limited representation in educational systems, public forums, and media. This lack of representation can create a sense of marginalization and hinder the spiritual growth of individuals seeking Pagan paths.

Creating safe spaces within communities, organizing public events, and spreading awareness through social media and other platforms can help address this challenge, fostering a more inclusive environment for Pagans.

Challenge: Balancing Modern Life with Pagan Practices

Navigating the demands of modern life while maintaining Pagan practices can be a significant challenge. Many Pagan traditions are deeply rooted in nature-based rituals, seasonal observances, and dedication to spiritual growth. However, the fast-paced nature of the modern world can make it challenging for individuals to find time for these practices.

Encouraging adaptability, offering guidance on incorporating Pagan practices into daily life, and emphasizing the importance of self-care can assist practitioners in finding a harmonious balance between their spiritual and mundane responsibilities.

As Paganism continues to gain recognition and understanding in the modern world, it faces various challenges and misconceptions that hinder its acceptance and growth. Addressing these challenges through education, advocacy, and fostering inclusive communities is essential for dispelling misconceptions and creating a supportive environment for Pagans.

By encouraging open dialogue, debunking common myths, and celebrating the diversity of Pagan paths, we can foster a greater understanding and appreciation for Paganism in the modern world.

Legal Issues and Religious Rights

Like any religion, Paganism can face legal challenges regarding the free exercise of religious rights and accommodation of its unique practices. This section aims to explore some common legal issues faced by Pagans and efforts taken to uphold their religious freedom while maintaining a harmonious society that respects diverse beliefs.

The Protection of Religious Freedom

In many countries, including the United States, religious freedom is a constitutionally protected right. The right to freely practice one's religion, without discrimination or undue interference from the government, is crucial for individuals to express their spirituality. However, Paganism, with its non-mainstream practices and rituals, has often struggled to obtain the same level of recognition as more established religions.

One significant legal issue that arises is the accommodation of Pagan religious practices within the framework of existing laws. For instance, Pagans may encounter challenges related to obtaining permits for outdoor rituals, accessing sacred sites, or religious headwear and symbols in workplaces or schools. Efforts are being made to establish legal precedents that recognize the significance of these practices and protect them under the umbrella of religious freedom.

Many Pagan traditions are nature-based and rely on access to natural landscapes for rituals and ceremonies. However, conflicts may arise when Pagans seek to utilize public or privately-owned lands for their religious practices. The legal framework must balance the rights of Pagans to access and utilize sacred sites with environmental and property rights concerns. Ongoing dialogue and cooperation between Pagans and relevant authorities can pave the way for fair resolutions.

Equal Treatment: Anti-Discrimination Laws

Discrimination against Pagans can manifest in various forms, such as employment, housing, or legal custody disputes. In response, anti-discrimination laws are evolving to include protections explicitly for religious minorities, including Pagans. Courts are increasingly recognizing and addressing cases where Pagans face prejudice or unequal treatment. The development of legal mechanisms and awareness campaigns can help combat discrimination and foster a society that embraces religious diversity.

Child Custody Battles

Custody battles involving Pagan parents can present unique legal challenges. In some cases, individuals have faced biased judgments due to misconceptions about Pagan practices. Courts are encouraged to consider the child's best interests when evaluating religious upbringing, in line with existing legal frameworks. Education campaigns, designed to dispel myths and provide accurate information about Paganism, can assist in ensuring fair and unbiased decisions in custody disputes.

Expressions of Religious Symbols

Paganism incorporates a diverse range of symbols and artifacts significant to individual paths and traditions. The issue of displaying or wearing such symbols in public spaces, workplaces, and schools can sometimes generate controversy. Striking a balance between freedom of religious expression and considerations of public perception is essential. Encouraging dialogue and education about

Paganism can help dispel misunderstandings and foster an inclusive environment for all religious symbols.

Challenges in Prison and Military Settings

Pagan inmates and military personnel, like individuals from other religious backgrounds, face obstacles in exercising their faith while within the confines of institutional structures. Efforts are being made to develop guidelines allowing Pagans to have access to relevant religious materials, participate in group rituals, and observe their holy days. Advocacy groups and legal experts work collaboratively to ensure that Pagans have equal opportunity to practice their faith while respecting security and operational considerations.

Acknowledging and embracing the religious rights of Pagans is crucial to nurturing a diverse and inclusive society that respects all faith traditions. While legal issues and challenges may arise, ongoing dialogue, education, and understanding pave the way forward.

As the legal framework continues to evolve, it is essential to ensure that Paganism and its followers are protected under the banner of religious freedom, fostering an environment where diversity thrives, and religious practices are celebrated.

Paganism's Influence on Art, Culture, and Environmental Activism

Throughout history, Pagan traditions have inspired artists, shaped cultural practices, and provided a foundation for environmental advocacy. This has resulted in a rich diversity of artistic expressions, cultural celebrations, and a profound sense of connection to the natural world.

Art has always been a mirror of society, reflecting its values and beliefs. Paganism, with its deep reverence for nature, has been a wellspring of inspiration for artists across different mediums. The Pagan worldview, which perceives the earth as a sacred entity, encourages a deep sense of communion with the natural world.

This connection often finds expression in paintings, sculptures, and installations that depict landscapes, animals, and mythological deities. Artists, such as the English painter John William Waterhouse, drew inspiration from Pagan myths and folklore to create stunning works of art that depicted gods and goddesses, nymphs, and other supernatural beings in lush natural settings.

Moreover, Pagan rituals and ceremonies have played a crucial role in shaping cultural practices. Pagan celebrations, such as the solstices and equinoxes, honor the cycles of nature and the changing seasons. These festivities have become a part of cultural heritage in many societies, with people coming together to celebrate and reconnect with nature. For example, the pagan festival of Beltane, celebrating the arrival of summer, has inspired modern cultural events like May Day parades and Maypole dancing in various European countries. Such demonstrations of cultural continuity foster a sense of community and a celebration of nature's cyclical rhythm.

In addition to its influence on art and cultural practices, Paganism has also made significant contributions to the realm of environmental activism. We know that Paganism recognizes the interconnectedness of all living beings and acknowledges the earth as a living organism deserving of respect and protection. This perspective has led many Pagans to become passionate environmental activists, working toward the preservation of natural landscapes and the sustainability of ecosystems.

One notable example is the earth-based spirituality movement, which draws on Pagan beliefs to foster a deep sense of ecological awareness and responsibility. Followers of this movement view the earth as a divine entity and advocate for sustainable practices, such as renewable energy, organic farming, and responsible consumption.

They combine spirituality and activism, organizing protests, engaging in reforestation initiatives, and supporting environmental organizations.

Furthermore, Paganism's belief in the sacredness of nature has influenced the practices and teachings of indigenous communities around the world. Indigenous cultures often embrace spiritual beliefs that prioritize the interconnectedness between humans and the natural world, emphasizing the need to live in harmony with the earth. By preserving their traditional practices and defending their ancestral lands, indigenous peoples contribute significantly to the global environmental movement. Their activism serves as a powerful reminder of the importance of maintaining a balanced relationship with the natural world and respecting its vast biodiversity.

CHAPTER 12

Paganism and Personal Growth

S teeped in ancient wisdom and rooted in an intricate connection with nature, Paganism offers a captivating path for those seeking personal transformation and spiritual exploration.

Unlocking the potential of Paganism as a vessel for self-growth means embracing the values of acceptance, respect, and empathy toward oneself and others. Along this exploratory path, we will discover the importance of balancing spirituality with everyday life, as well as how Paganism can be used for healing and transformation.

Self-Discovery through Pagan Practices

Embracing a variety of ancient traditions and spiritualities, Pagans can tap into the wisdom of the ages to embark on a profound journey of personal exploration and understanding. Let's explore how Paganism can help practitioners ignite the flame of self-discovery within.

Connecting with Nature

At the heart of Paganism lies a deep reverence for nature and the natural world. By immersing oneself in the beauty and rhythms of nature, Pagans can open themselves up to transformative experiences.

Whether it is spending time in the serene embrace of a forest, walking along a sandy beach, or meditating near a flowing river, Pagans can connect with the earth's boundless energy and find solace, inspiration, and meaning. These experiences in nature can awaken a sense of wonderment, triggering self-reflection and fostering a deeper understanding of oneself within the grand tapestry of life.

Rituals and Ceremonies

Rituals and ceremonies offer a structured framework for self-discovery. Through the creation of sacred spaces, the practice of meditation, or the casting of a circle, Pagans can enter into a state of heightened awareness, creating opportunities for self-exploration.

These rituals can act as a mirror, reflecting our desires, fears, and beliefs, allowing us to peel back the layers of our being and confront our true selves. Whether performed alone or within a community, these ceremonies provide a sacred container for personal discovery and growth.

Archetypes and Mythology

The diverse pantheons and mythologies embraced by Paganism offer a treasure trove of archetypal figures and stories that mirror the human experience. Exploring these mythologies can serve as a gateway to understanding our own narratives and psyche. From the fierce warrior to the wise crone, the mischievous trickster to the nurturing mother, each archetype holds lessons and insights that resonate within us.

By delving into these stories and identifying the archetypes that speak to them, Pagans can uncover hidden aspects of their own personalities, discovering newfound strengths, and integrating them into their lives.

Divination and Intuition

Divination, the practice of seeking guidance or insight from spiritual sources, is a powerful tool for self-discovery embraced by many Pagans. Whether through tarot cards, runes, scrying, or other divination methods, Pagans can tap into their intuition and access deeper levels of self-awareness.

Through divination, answers to questions that perplex the conscious mind can be revealed, shedding light on unresolved issues, or pointing toward new paths of personal growth. This process of seeking divine or higher guidance reinforces the belief in one's own inner wisdom and strengthens the connection to the spiritual realm.

Shadow Work and Personal Transformation

Paganism acknowledges that the journey of self-discovery often entails confronting one's shadows—those hidden aspects of ourselves that we may fear or deny. Through embracing the concept of shadow work, Pagans delve into the depths of their psyches, exploring areas of pain, trauma, and unresolved emotions.

By courageously facing and integrating these shadow aspects, individuals can experience personal transformation and growth. The shadows become stepping stones toward greater self-acceptance and wholeness, forming a solid foundation for self-discovery.

By embracing these elements, Pagans embark on a transformative journey that uncovers the layers of their being, leading to greater self-awareness, personal growth, and alignment with their true purpose. The power of Paganism lies in its ability to provide a sacred framework for self-discovery, uplifting and guiding individuals on their quest to live authentic, fulfilling lives.

Healing and Transformation

Paganism encompasses a rich tapestry of beliefs and practices that foster personal growth, self-discovery, and healing. In this section, let's take a look at how Pagans can utilize the various aspects of their faith to facilitate healing and transformation.

Natural Connections

As with self-development, at the heart of Paganism lies a reverence for the natural world. Pagans recognize the divine in all forms of life and understand the interconnectedness of the universe.

By immersing themselves in nature, Pagans can experience a profound sense of healing and transformation. Taking walks in the forest, meditating by a river, or even gardening can help rejuvenate the spirit and foster a sense of oneness with the earth.

Seeking Spiritual Guidance

Paganism offers a vast array of deities, spirits, and guides that can serve as sources of inspiration and healing. Pagans often establish relationships with these beings through prayer, meditation, and offerings.

By seeking spiritual guidance and connecting with these divine entities, followers can receive wisdom, healing energy, and support during challenging times. Shamanic practices, such as journeying or trancework, can also be utilized to access the spiritual realms and gain insights for personal transformation.

Rituals and Ceremonies

Cleansing rituals, such as smudging or purifying baths, can help release negativity and promote emotional healing. Full moon ceremonies are often used to manifest desires and intentions, while seasonal celebrations provide opportunities for personal growth and renewal.

Divination and Self-Reflection

Divination tools, such as tarot cards, runes, or scrying, can enable Pagans to gain insights into their lives, explore their subconscious minds, and identify areas in need of healing and transformation.

Through divination, individuals can uncover hidden patterns, gain clarity, and receive guidance for their personal journeys. Self-reflection practices, such as journaling or meditation, further facilitate growth by fostering self-awareness and understanding.

Energy and Chakra Work

Paganism acknowledges the existence and manipulation of energy, emphasizing the importance of balanced energies for overall well-being. Chakra work, a practice derived from Eastern spirituality but embraced by many Pagans, involves aligning and harmonizing the energy centers in the body.

Through chakra meditations, energy healing techniques, and visualizations, individuals can address emotional blockages, release stagnant energy, and cultivate a sense of empowerment and vitality.

Ancestral Connections

Many Pagans honor their ancestors and recognize their role in shaping their present lives. By acknowledging and connecting with ancestral energies, individuals can tap into a wellspring of wisdom, strength, and guidance.

Ancestor altars, ancestral prayers, and rituals performed to honor and remember one's lineage can provide a deep sense of healing and transformation. Exploring family history, genealogy, and cultural traditions further deepens this connection to the past.

Balancing Spirituality With Everyday Life

Living a spiritual life is a deeply personal journey, and for those who practice Paganism, finding ways to balance their spirituality with the demands of everyday life can be a beautiful and transformative experience. Incorporating Pagan rituals and spells into daily routines can provide a sense of grounding, connection, and empowerment.

Let's explore various methods to help Pagans find equilibrium between their spiritual practices and the practicalities of everyday life.

Setting Intentions and Mindful Awareness

One of the fundamental aspects of incorporating Paganism into daily life lies in setting intentions and being mindfully aware of our actions. Pagans can begin each day by setting an intention that aligns with their spiritual beliefs—a simple affirmation or statement that resonates with their innermost desires. By doing so, they infuse their everyday actions with spiritual significance and create a harmonious connection between their beliefs and the world around them.

Rituals for Morning and Evening

Designing daily rituals can help Pagans maintain a spiritual connection throughout the day. In the morning, establish a simple ritual that can include lighting a candle, reciting a blessing, or setting an intention for the day. This prompts a mindful start, grounding followers in their beliefs before the demands of daily life take over.

Similarly, adopting an evening ritual can help with winding down, reflecting, and reconnecting with their spirituality. Pagans may light some incense, create a sacred space, or engage in a short meditation to create a sense of closure for the day. This ritual can also involve gratitude expression for the blessings and lessons received throughout the day.

Incorporating Nature into Everyday Life

Many Pagans find solace and connection with the natural world, considering it sacred and divine. Finding ways to incorporate nature into daily life can help strengthen this connection. Many followers spend time outdoors, even if it's just a short walk in a nearby park and take a moment to appreciate the beauty and serenity of nature. Others cultivate a herb garden or surround themselves with houseplants to create a nurturing environment that reflects their Pagan beliefs.

Attuning to the Seasons and Moon Phases

Paganism is often strongly connected to the cycles of nature. By paying attention to the changing seasons and moon phases, Pagans can integrate their spiritual practices more deeply into everyday life.

Followers take note of solstices, equinoxes, and significant lunar events such as full moons and new moons. They then utilize these moments to perform rituals or spells that correspond with the energy of the current season or moon phase.

Infusing Daily Activities with Purpose

Everyday activities can become rituals in themselves when approached with intention and purpose. Cooking, for example, can be transformed into a sacred act by using locally sourced produce, blessing ingredients, or dedicating the act of nourishment to deities or spiritual beliefs.

Other routines like bathing, cleaning, or even commuting can also be infused with spirituality if done mindfully and with focused intent.

Carrying Symbols and Charms

Symbolism plays a significant role in Paganism, and for followers, carrying physical symbols or charms can serve as constant reminders of their spiritual path. They can choose items that resonate with their beliefs, such as crystals, amulets, or talismans, and keep them close throughout the day. These tangible objects can serve as a source of strength, protection, and connection to their spiritual practice.

Balancing spirituality and everyday life is not an exact science but a personal journey. By incorporating Pagan rituals and spells into their daily routines, Pagans create opportunities to weave their spiritual beliefs seamlessly into the fabric of their lives.

Everyday acts can hold great significance when performed with intention and mindful awareness.

CHAPTER 13

Paganism and the Environment

At its core, Paganism embraces a reverence for the natural world, recognizing that every tree, every creature, and every gust of wind carries a divinity within. Paganism, in its diverse forms, draws inspiration from the wisdom and rhythms of nature, urging us to forge a more harmonious connection with our Earth.

Paganism also recognizes the intrinsic value of the earth as a nurturing and life-sustaining force. Through this belief system, we are reminded of our responsibility to treat the environment with respect, understanding that our actions ripple through the intricate web of life. By embodying principles of sustainability, compassion, and stewardship, Pagans seek to cultivate a profound love for nature and an unwavering commitment to protect it.

In this chapter, we will explore the ways in which Pagan practices contribute to environmental sustainability, looking at the ancient rituals preserved over time and the innovative approaches embraced by modern Pagans.

Eco-Spirituality and Earth Stewardship

Eco-spirituality and earth stewardship are fundamental aspects of Paganism, connecting practitioners with the natural world and emphasizing the importance of living in harmony with the earth.

In this section, let's delve deeper into the principles and practices of eco-spirituality and earth stewardship within the Pagan community.

Paganism recognizes the earth as a sacred and living entity, often referred to as Gaia or Mother Earth. The belief in the immanent divinity of nature forms the foundation of eco-spirituality within Paganism. This perspective fosters a deep reverence and respect for the natural world, understanding that all elements, including plants, animals, and ecosystems, have inherent value and are integral to the interconnected web of life.

Pagan rituals often take place outdoors, in natural settings such as forests, meadows, or by bodies of water. Gathering in these spaces allows Pagans to forge a deep connection with the earth, forming a direct bond with the energy and wisdom of the natural world. By immersing themselves in the beauty and tranquility of nature, Pagans believe they can tap into a spiritual energy that rejuvenates and nurtures both their souls and the earth itself.

Of course, we also have the Wheel of the Year. The Pagan calendar revolves around the sacred Wheel of the Year, which consists of eight holidays (Sabbats) that celebrate the changing seasons and agricultural cycles. These Sabbats, such as Samhain, Beltane, and the Summer Solstice, mark important milestones in the earth's cycle and provide opportunities for spiritual reflection, gratitude, and deep connection with the natural rhythms of life. Additionally, the observance of these holidays encourages Pagans to be mindful of the changing seasons and to develop a sense of harmony with the earth and its cycles.

Additionally, rituals in Paganism often incorporate elements of nature, such as stones, crystals, herbs, and sacred water, to honor and tap into the earth's energy. These rituals can range from simple acts of gratitude, like leaving offerings in natural spaces, to more elaborate ceremonies that honor specific deities or natural phenomena. By engaging in these practices, Pagans aim to cultivate a deeper understanding of their role as stewards of the earth and to foster a sense of responsibility for its care.

Environmental Activism and Earth Stewardship

Paganism places a strong emphasis on environmental activism and taking concrete actions to protect and restore the earth. Many Pagans identify as environmentalists and actively engage in initiatives that address issues such as climate change, habitat destruction, and pollution.

Earth stewardship is seen as a sacred duty, embodying the principles of eco-spirituality. Practices such as sustainable living, organic gardening, and supporting local and eco-friendly businesses are embraced as ways to reduce one's ecological footprint and contribute to the well-being of the earth.

Sacred Ecology

Sacred ecology is a branch of eco-spirituality within Paganism that explores the interconnectedness of all beings and the concept of environmental holism. It recognizes that harm to one part of the ecosystem affects the whole, and thus, maintaining the well-being of the earth necessitates a holistic approach.

This perspective encourages practitioners to reshape their worldview and lifestyle to align with the principles of sustainability and interconnectedness. By embracing sacred ecology, Pagans seek to heal the disconnection between humans and nature and work toward building a more harmonious and regenerative relationship with the earth.

Rituals and Practices for Honoring Nature

Central to Paganism is the concept of honoring and revering nature as sacred. Through various rituals and practices, Pagans celebrate the cycles of life, express gratitude, and seek harmony with the natural elements. Let's take a look at some of the key rituals and practices utilized by Pagans to honor nature and deepen their connection with the natural world.

Seasonal Celebrations

One of the cornerstones of Paganism is the celebration of the changing seasons. Pagans pay homage to the earth's natural cycles through the four major seasonal celebrations known as Sabbats.

Moon Rituals

Pagans view the moon as a powerful celestial symbol that influences various aspects of life. Moon rituals are a common practice to harness the moon's energy and align with its cycles. Some common moon rituals in Paganism include:

- **Full Moon Rituals:** During the full moon, Pagans often gather to pay respects to its illuminated beauty. They may perform rituals involving meditation, divination, and spellcasting, focusing on intentions relating to personal growth, healing, and wisdom.

- **New Moon Rituals:** The new moon represents beginnings and offers an opportunity to set new intentions. Pagans engage in rituals involving journaling, visualization, or candle magic to manifest desires, release old patterns, and embark on fresh endeavors.

Sacred Sites Pilgrimage

Many Pagans hold a deep connection to sacred sites in nature. These sites, such as stone circles, ancient forests, or natural landmarks, are believed to hold spiritual power.

Pagan practitioners often embark on pilgrimages to these locations as a means of connecting with the energy of the land, ancestors, and deity. These journeys involve rituals of offering, meditation, and contemplation to foster a stronger bond with the natural world.

Elemental Rituals

Pagans recognize the importance of the elements—earth, air, fire, and water—as vital forces that sustain life. Rituals that invoke and honor these elements are prevalent among Pagan practitioners.

These rituals involve paying homage to each element individually, utilizing corresponding symbols, tools, and offerings. For example, earth rituals may involve burying seeds or crystals, air rituals may incorporate incense or feathers, fire rituals may use flames or candles, and water rituals may include immersing oneself in natural bodies of water or offering libations.

In Paganism, rituals and practices centered around honoring nature play a significant role in maintaining a harmonious connection with the natural world. Seasonal celebrations, moon rituals, sacred sites pilgrimages, and elemental rituals are just a few examples of the various ways Pagans honor and celebrate the sacredness of the earth. By engaging in these rituals, Pagans deepen their spirituality, enhance their gratitude for the environment, and cultivate a greater sense of interconnectedness with the natural world.

Chapter 14

Exploring Deeper Paths

In recent years, the ancient traditions and wisdom of Paganism have experienced a resurgence, attracting individuals seeking a deeper connection with nature, spirituality, and self. As practitioners delve further into the Pagan path, a desire for advanced studies arises, fostering personal growth and the refinement of their practice.

If you have read this book so far and you're keen to learn more about Paganism, here are some tips to help you delve deeper into this ancient belief system.

Deepening Your Understanding

At the core of advanced studies in Paganism lies a thirst for knowledge and a desire to delve deeper into the various traditions and belief systems. By expanding your understanding of different Pagan paths, such as Wicca, Druidry, or Heathenry, you can gain a broader perspective and appreciation of the diverse practices within the Pagan community.

Engage in extensive reading, attend workshops, participate in online forums and local gatherings, and seek out experienced mentors who can guide you through this journey of exploration and learning.

Developing Mastery of Ritual and Magick

Advanced Pagans often seek to refine their skillset by gaining a deeper understanding of rituals, spellcasting, and magickal practices. Delve into the study of correspondences, symbolism, and the energetic principles that underpin magickal workings.

Explore the realms of elemental magick, creating sacred space, and working with deities and spirits. Consider connecting with established covens, circles, or Pagan organizations that offer advanced training in ritual and magick to develop a greater mastery of these arts.

Exploring Esoteric and Mystery Traditions

For those seeking a more mysterious and mystical path, delving into esoteric and mystery traditions can provide profound insights and transformative experiences. Study and practice the magical systems such as the Western Mystery Tradition, Hermeticism, Kabbalah, or Alchemy.

These disciplines offer a deeper exploration of symbolism, metaphysics, and spiritual transformation, enhancing and integrating with Pagan practices. Engage in studies, find respected teachers, and explore ancient texts to unravel the mysteries within these rich traditions.

Deepening Your Connection with Nature

Explore the cycles of the moon, the changing seasons, and celestial movements. Dedicate time to communing with spirits of nature, whether through solitary meditation or participating in outdoor rituals. By deepening this connection, you can tap into profound wisdom and develop a greater appreciation for the sacredness of all living things.

Cultivating Inner Spiritual Practices

Beyond external rituals and practices, advanced Pagan studies often involve cultivating inner spiritual practices for personal growth and transformation. This includes meditation, energy work, shadow work, dream recall, and exploring altered states of consciousness.

Develop a regular meditation practice and explore various techniques such as visualization, breathwork, or chanting. Engage in journaling and self-reflection to uncover deeper aspects of your spiritual journey. By connecting with your inner self, you can access profound insights and develop a more balanced and harmonious approach to your practice.

Sharing Your Wisdom

Advanced studies in Paganism often lead practitioners to take on leadership roles within the community or to become teachers in their own right. Embrace the opportunity to share your knowledge and experiences by mentoring others, creating workshops, or writing books.

Engaging in teaching or public speaking can not only enhance your understanding but also provide opportunities for personal growth and transformation. By sharing your wisdom, you contribute to the growth and enrichment of the Pagan community itself.

Advanced studies in Paganism present a vast array of opportunities for personal growth and spiritual development. Remember, the Pagan journey is an ongoing process of learning and self-discovery, and embracing advanced studies leads to a greater appreciation of the interconnectedness of all things and facilitates personal transformation and enlightenment.

Initiatory Traditions and Mystery Schools

Initiatory Traditions, often referred to as "mystery traditions," are rooted in ancient practices that were passed down through generations of practitioners. These traditions focus on inner transformation, personal exploration, and seeking a deeper understanding of the mysteries of existence. Initiatory Traditions are seen as a journey, a gradual unveiling of knowledge and wisdom that unfolds over time through a series of initiation ceremonies and rituals.

The concept of initiation is central to these traditions. Initiation is a sacred rite of passage that represents an individual's commitment to their path and their willingness to undergo transformative experiences. It is an opportunity for self-discovery, personal growth, and connecting with the divine. Through these initiation ceremonies, practitioners are guided into the mysteries of their chosen tradition, unlocking deeper layers of spiritual insight, and understanding.

Mystery Schools, on the other hand, are institutions or organizations that offer structured education and training in esoteric knowledge and wisdom. These schools cultivate an environment for seekers to engage in learning, reflection, and practical application of spiritual teachings. Mystery Schools provide a framework for students to delve into the mysteries of existence, explore metaphysical concepts, develop their spiritual practices, and foster a deeper connection with the divine.

The curriculum of Mystery Schools varies depending on the tradition or lineage they belong to. Some schools focus on astrology, divination, herbalism, or magic, while others delve into the realms of shamanism, sacred geometry, alchemy, or mythological studies. The purpose of these schools is not only to impart knowledge but also to provide a supportive community for students to cultivate their spiritual gifts and talents.

One of the fascinating aspects of Initiatory Traditions and Mystery Schools is their emphasis on direct experience and personal connection with the divine. Unlike mainstream religions that often rely on an intermediary figure, these traditions encourage practitioners to establish a direct relationship with the spiritual realms. This emphasis on personal gnosis allows individuals to develop their unique spiritual path, honoring their own experiences and insights.

Initiatory Traditions and Mystery Schools also value the preservation of ancient wisdom and lineage teachings. Many of these traditions trace their origins back to pre-Christian times and have been passed down through select individuals or lineages. This lineage gives these traditions a sense of continuity and a connection to the ancient past. The teachings and practices are held as sacred and are carefully handed down to initiates who are deemed ready to receive them.

Membership in these traditions and schools typically requires a commitment to the path, a willingness to undergo a period of study and preparation, and participation in initiation rites. The initiation rituals are often shrouded in secrecy to preserve the transformative power of the experience. While some information about these traditions and schools may be accessible to the public, the deeper mysteries are revealed only to those who have undergone the initiatory process.

The journey within Initiatory Traditions and Mystery Schools is not just about acquiring knowledge but also about personal transformation. The rituals, practices, and teachings aim to awaken the individual to their true nature, helping them discover their unique spiritual gifts and unleash their full potential. The journey is often challenging, requiring dedication, discipline, and a willingness to confront inner shadows, and limiting beliefs. However, the rewards of such dedication can be profound, resulting in personal growth, expanded consciousness, and a deep sense of purpose and fulfillment.

Specialized Practices – Shamanism and Kitchen Witchery

Within the broad umbrella of Paganism, there are specialized practices that hold unique significance and serve different purposes for practitioners. In this section, let's focus on two specific branches—Shamanism and Kitchen Witchery.

Shamanism

Shamanism is an ancient spiritual practice that can be found across various cultures worldwide. It involves connecting with the spirit world and harnessing the power of nature and spirits for healing, guidance, and personal transformation. Key elements of Shamanism include shamanic journeying, soul retrieval, and working with spirit allies.

Shamanic Journeying

At the heart of Shamanism lies the practice of shamanic journeying, wherein a practitioner enters an altered state of consciousness, often through drumming or other rhythmic methods, to seek visions and wisdom from the spirit realm. Through journeying, shamans explore different realms, interact with spirit guides, animals, ancestors, and receive messages and healing.

Soul Retrieval

Another crucial aspect of Shamanism is soul retrieval. It is believed that when a person experiences trauma, a part of their soul may become fragmented or lost. A shaman uses various techniques to journey into the spirit world, locate and retrieve these lost soul fragments, and reintegrate them with the individual, facilitating healing and wholeness.

Working with Spirit Allies

Shamans establish relationships with various spirit allies, such as power animals, plant spirits, and ancestors. These allies offer guidance, protection, and support during shamanic practices and rituals. Working with their spirit allies, shamans can access powerful energies and ancient wisdom to address specific issues and bring healing to themselves or others.

Kitchen Witchery

Kitchen Witchery is a specialized practice within Paganism that revolves around magickal workings, rituals, and traditions centered within the domestic sphere. It emphasizes the use of everyday items found in the kitchen, such as herbs, oils, and utensils, to create magickal recipes, potions, and spells.

The kitchen itself becomes a sacred space where intentions are set, and the act of cooking and nurturing takes on a deeper spiritual significance.

Herblore and Spellcasting

Central to Kitchen Witchery is the use of herbs and plants for healing, protection, and magickal purposes. From drying herbs in the kitchen to creating herb bundles, potions, and spell jars, Kitchen Witches imbue their craft with the power of nature. These spellcasting practices range from cooking with intention, creating herbal remedies, and crafting charms to bring about specific outcomes or blessings.

The Kitchen as a Sacred Space

The domestic kitchen is considered a sacred space in Kitchen Witchery. It is seen as a place where meals are prepared with love and nurturing energies, and where the elements of fire, water, earth, and air come together in harmonious balance. Kitchen Witches infuse their cooking with mindfulness, ensuring that every ingredient is chosen consciously, and every act is performed with intention.

Cycles and Rituals

Kitchen Witchery emphasizes honoring the cycles of nature and the seasons. The Wheel of the Year, which includes Sabbats such as Samhain and Beltane, plays an essential role in guiding Kitchen Witch rituals and celebrations.

During these special times, elaborate feasts are prepared, ancient rituals are performed, and blessings are called upon to harmonize with the natural rhythms of the earth.

Amongst the different types of Paganism, Shamanism and Kitchen Witchery stand out as specialized practices that enhance and deepen spiritual experiences. While Shamanism brings practitioners closer to the spirit world, facilitating healing and transformation, Kitchen Witchery allows individuals to infuse their everyday lives with magick, love, and intention using common household tools and practices.

Both practices offer unique pathways for personal growth, exploration, and connection to the natural and spiritual realms. Through Shamanism and Kitchen Witchery, followers can tap into the ancient wisdom embedded in these specialized Pagan practices, ultimately fostering a deeper connection with themselves, their communities, and the divine.

CHAPTER 15

Living a Pagan Life

A s we reach the final chapter of this book on understanding Paganism, it is only fitting that we explore the concept of living a Pagan life. Throughout this journey, we have delved into the history, beliefs, and practices of this ancient and diverse spiritual path. Now, it is time to take that knowledge and embark upon a personal exploration of what it truly means to be a Pagan in the modern world.

Living a Pagan life is not merely about attending rituals or studying ancient texts; it is a holistic way of being, a perennial celebration of the interconnectedness of all things. It is about living in harmony with nature, recognizing the divine in every aspect of existence, and embracing the cycles of life and death with reverence and awe.

Living a Pagan life does not require adherence to a specific set of rules or dogmas. Instead, it encourages individuality and personal connection with the divine. Whether you are drawn to the mystical traditions of Wicca, the earth-centered spirituality of Druidry, or any of the countless other paths within Paganism, this chapter will provide you with insights and practical suggestions to infuse your daily life with spiritual meaning and purpose.

Small Steps to Begin Integrating Pagan Beliefs Into Your Daily Life

If you are interested in integrating Pagan beliefs into your daily life, here are some small steps you can take to embark on this journey:

Research and Understand Paganism

Begin by educating yourself about the different branches of Paganism, such as Wicca, Druidry, and Heathenry. Read books, join online forums, and attend local Pagan events to gain a deeper understanding of the core beliefs, practices, and customs associated with Paganism.

Find Your Connection with Nature

Connecting with nature is at the heart of Pagan spirituality. Spend time outdoors, whether it's in a park, a forest, or your own garden. Engage your senses by noticing the sounds, smells, and textures around you. Develop a practice of grounding yourself by standing barefoot on the earth, feeling its energy flow through you.

Create an Altar

Setting up an altar can serve as a focal point for your Pagan practices and beliefs. Choose a dedicated space, large or small, where you can display objects that are meaningful to you. These objects might include crystals, feathers, shells, images of deities or nature, and candles. Arrange them with intention and personalize your altar to reflect your spiritual journey.

Start a Daily Ritual

Rituals can be simple or elaborate, depending on your preferences. Begin by setting a specific time each day to connect with your spirituality. Light a candle, offer a prayer, or meditate to create a sacred space in which you can attune to the Divine or commune with nature. Gradually, you can expand and deepen your ritual practice.

Celebrate the Wheel of the Year

The Pagan Wheel of the Year marks the changing seasons and the turning of the earth. Each season has its corresponding Sabbat, which represents different aspects of life and nature. Start by recognizing and celebrating the solstices and equinoxes, such as Yule, Ostara, Litha, and Mabon. These celebrations can be as simple as preparing a special meal, decorating your altar, or spending time in nature, honoring the specific energies of the season.

Work with the Elements

Paganism often emphasizes the power of the elements (earth, air, water, fire) and their energies. Take time to connect with each element through simple practices. For Earth, spend time gardening or burying a crystal in the ground. Light incense or a feather to connect with Air. Create a bonfire or work with candles in your rituals to honor Fire. Use water in a ritual bath or spend time by a body of water to connect with the element of Water. Lastly, reflect and meditate on the element of Spirit, recognizing the divine sacredness in all things.

Develop a Daily Meditation Practice

Meditation is a powerful tool for centering your mind, body, and spirit. Set aside a few minutes each day to sit in quiet reflection. Focus on your breath and allow thoughts to pass without judgment. You can also incorporate visualization techniques, such as imagining yourself surrounded by nature or communing with your chosen deities. Experiment with different meditation practices to find what resonates with you.

Honor Ancestors and Deities

Connect with your ancestors by creating a dedicated space or remembrance, such as a picture or small memento, where you can express gratitude and seek guidance. Research different Pagan deities and identify those that align with your beliefs. Build relationships with these deities through offerings, prayers, and rituals. Remember to approach them with respect and an open heart.

Explore Divination Tools

Divination tools, such as tarot cards, runes, or pendulums, can be utilized to gain insight and guidance on your spiritual journey. Choose a tool that resonates with you and take the time to study its symbolism, meanings, and interpretations. Practice regularly to develop your intuition and deepen your connection with the spiritual realm.

Join a Pagan Community

Finally, consider joining a local or online Pagan community. Engaging with like-minded individuals can provide support, guidance, and opportunities to learn from others' experiences. Attend workshops, rituals, or circles to deepen your understanding and find belonging within the Pagan community.

Remember, integrating Pagan beliefs into your daily life is a personal journey. These small steps can serve as a starting point, but always trust your intuition and follow what feels right for you. Let the wisdom of nature guide you as you cultivate a meaningful and fulfilling spiritual practice.

Finding Your Own Path Within Paganism

Finding your own path within Paganism is a personal journey that involves self-discovery, exploration, and the uncovering of hidden truths. In this section, we will delve into the ways you can navigate and carve your unique path within this diverse and inclusive spiritual tradition.

Self-Reflection and Exploration

The first step in finding your own path within Paganism is to engage in self-reflection and exploration. Take the time to understand your own beliefs, values, and spiritual inclinations.

Ask yourself important questions about your views on nature, divinity, ethics, and rituals. Consider what resonates with you and what you are drawn to. Reflecting on your experiences, past influences, and the elements of various Pagan traditions that appeal to you can provide valuable insights into your own path within the larger tapestry of Paganism.

Research and Study

To deepen your understanding of Paganism and its diverse practices, engage in research and study. There are countless books, websites, and online communities dedicated to Paganism that can provide a wealth of information.

Seek out reputable sources, both historical and contemporary, to learn about different Pagan paths, traditions, and deities. Reading and absorbing various perspectives will broaden your horizons and help you identify aspects that resonate with your own spiritual journey.

Connect with a Community

Engaging with a community of like-minded individuals can be a transformative experience. Attend Pagan events, workshops, and festivals to connect with others who share your interests. Join online forums and social media groups dedicated to Paganism to engage in discussions and seek advice.

Connecting with a supportive community can provide guidance, encouragement, and a sense of belonging as you navigate your own path. Remember, however, that while community support is valuable, it is also important to maintain your own unique perspective and not feel pressured to conform to others' beliefs or practices.

Practice and Experiment

Exploring various rituals, practices, and traditions is an important part of finding your own path within Paganism. Engage in experimentation and try different rituals, meditation techniques, and divination methods. Listen to your intuition and pay attention to what brings you a sense of peace, connection, and spiritual fulfillment.

Don't be afraid to create your own rituals, symbols, correspondences, or ceremonies based on what resonates with you personally. Embrace the freedom and flexibility that Paganism offers to honor nature and the divine in a way that feels authentic and true to your spirit.

Seek Guidance from Mentors

Finding a mentor or someone more experienced in Paganism can provide invaluable guidance and support as you continue your spiritual journey. A mentor can share their experiences, suggest resources, and help you navigate through any challenges you may encounter.

Seek authentic connections with individuals who resonate with you on a spiritual level and whose values align with your own. Remember that each person's path is unique, and their experiences may not mirror your own. Use them as a guide, but ultimately trust yourself and your own inner wisdom.

Embrace Eclecticism

Paganism is an eclectic spiritual tradition that encompasses myriad beliefs and practices. Embrace the freedom to draw inspiration and wisdom from multiple sources.

As you explore various traditions, deities, and rituals, you may find that your path within Paganism is an amalgamation of different influences. Don't be confined by labels or limit yourself to a single tradition. Let your path unfold organically, incorporating elements that speak to your heart and resonates with your truth.

Remember that your path is unique, and it is essential to trust your own inner wisdom. Keep seeking, learning, and evolving, as your path within Paganism unfolds into a beautiful tapestry woven with your own experiences, beliefs, and spiritual connection to nature and the divine.

Continuing the Journey of Understanding and Growth

As we reach the conclusion of this book, it is important to remember that the journey of understanding and growth does not end here. In fact, this is just the beginning. With every turn of the page, new insights and discoveries have revealed themselves, and we have explored the rich tapestry of beliefs, practices, and traditions that make up this diverse and vibrant path. But the beauty of Paganism lies in its ever-evolving nature, constantly inviting us to explore deeper, question further, and embrace new perspectives.

To be a new Pagan today is to embody an awakening, a willingness to step outside of societal norms and find connection with the natural world, the divine, and one's own inner self. It is a journey that requires courage, curiosity, and a genuine desire to learn. With each step we take along this path, we discover that we are not alone. We join a community of kindred spirits, a network of individuals who, like us, seek a connection to something greater than themselves.

Central to our continued growth as new Pagans is the practice of continuous learning. While books like this provide a valuable foundation, they are only the tip of the iceberg. Paganism is an experiential path, where knowledge is gained through our interactions with nature, the seasons, and the deities we choose to honor. It is through direct experiences and personal encounters that we truly come to understand the intricate web of life that surrounds us.

One of the first steps in our ongoing journey is the exploration of the core beliefs within Paganism. As new Pagans, we have likely been drawn to this path due to our shared affinity for nature, reverence for the cycles of life, and a sense of the divine within all things.

Yet, it is important to recognize that there is no one-size-fits-all. Paganism is diverse, and each practitioner brings their own unique perspective and interpretation to their spiritual practice.

Thus, as new Pagans, it becomes essential to study and explore the wide variety of traditions and practices that fall under the umbrella of Paganism. Whether it's Wicca, Druidry, Heathenry, or any of the other countless paths, each has its own wisdom to offer. By embracing this diversity, we broaden our understanding of the interconnectedness of all things and gain a deeper appreciation for the vast tapestry of human spiritual experience.

However, understanding alone is not enough. It is equally important to put our newfound knowledge into practice. Here, rituals and ceremonies become the heart of our spiritual journey. Whether it is celebrating the turning of the seasons, performing spells for healing and manifestation, or communing with deities and spirits, these sacred acts connect us to the divine and provide a space for growth and transformation.

While rituals and ceremonies are undoubtedly powerful tools, it is essential to approach them with intention and respect. Building a daily practice allows us to establish a harmonious connection with the divine and weave our spirituality into the tapestry of our everyday lives. From morning meditations to divination practices, or even simply taking walks in nature, these small moments of mindfulness and reverence invite us to experience the sacred in the ordinary.

In addition to personal experiences, the Pagan community plays a vital role in our continued growth as individuals and as a collective. It is within the community that we find support, guidance, and inspiration. Seek out like-minded individuals, whether through local meet-ups, online forums, or workshops and festivals. Engage, share, and learn from others, for it is through these interactions that we truly thrive.

Furthermore, it is important to acknowledge the responsibility we have as new Pagans to actively contribute to the growth and understanding of our path. Share your knowledge, whether through teaching, writing, or simply engaging in meaningful conversations. The act of articulating our own beliefs helps us deepen our understanding and solidify our personal practice. By giving back to the community, we foster an environment where new seekers can find the guidance and support they need.

As you embark on this journey of understanding and growth as a new Pagan, always remember to approach it with an open heart and an open mind. Be patient with yourself, for growth takes time. Cherish the connections you make, both with the divine and with your fellow practitioners. Embrace the challenges and setbacks, for they offer valuable opportunities for learning and growth.

Above all, let love and kindness guide you along this path. In all that you do, strive to act with compassion and empathy, not only toward those who share your beliefs but toward all living beings. Paganism teaches us to honor the sacredness of life, and by embodying these values, we become co-creators of a more inclusive, harmonious, and interconnected world.

References

BBC - Religion: Paganism. (n.d.). https://www.bbc.co.uk/religion/religions/paganism/

Composanto, J. (2022, March 30). A Non-Pagan's Guide to Understanding Modern Paganism. *Medium*. https://medium.com/world-tree-heritage/a-non-pagans-guide-to-understanding-modern-paganism-6ee0cd3591fa

INFOGRAPHIC: Wicca, Druidry, paganism, Asatru, what are they? | Washington State Department of Corrections. (n.d.). https://www.doc.wa.gov/docs/publications/infographics/100-PO047.htm

Joralemon, D. (2001). Shamanism. In *Elsevier eBooks* (pp. 14032–14035). https://doi.org/10.1016/b0-08-043076-7/00952-9

Lesso, R. (2024, March 13). *What is Pagan Religion?* TheCollector. https://www.thecollector.com/what-is-pagan-religion/

MacIntyre, C. (2023, March 22). Paganism is on the rise—here's where to discover its traditions. *Culture*. https://www.nationalgeographic.com/culture/article/where-to-go-to-explore-pagan-culture

Scottish Pagan Federation. (2023, May 14). *Pagan Traditions - Scottish Pagan Federation*. https://scottishpf.org/pagan-traditions/

Swan, S., & Swan, S. (2023, November 9). *The Wheel of the Year, explained*. Sea Witch Botanicals. https://seawitchbotanicals.com/blogs/swb/the-wheel-of-the-year-explained

The Economist. (2023, February 9). Shamanism is Britain's fastest-growing religion. *The Economist*. https://www.economist.com/britain/2023/02/09/shamanism-is-britains-fastest-growing-religion?utm_medium=cpc.adword.

pd&utm_source=google&ppccampaignID=18151738051&ppcadID=&utm_campaign=a.22brand_pmax&utm_content=conversion.direct-response.anonymous&gad_source=1&gclid=EAIaIQobChMI1q_LgqaLhgMVlguiAx1fQgwxEAAYASAAEgKdgfD_BwE&gclsrc=aw.ds

The Wheel of the Year: the calendar of pagan festivals explained. (n.d.). Sky HISTORY TV Channel. https://www.history.co.uk/articles/the-wheel-of-the-year-the-calendar-of-pagan-festivals-explained

What do pagans do? (n.d.). The Pluralism Project. https://pluralism.org/what-do-pagans-do

What is Wicca? An expert on modern witchcraft explains. | BrandeisNOW. (n.d.). BrandeisNOW. https://www.brandeis.edu/now/2021/september/wicca-berger-conversation.html

White, E. D. (2024, March 29). *Paganism | Definition, Beliefs, Origin, & Christianity.* Encyclopedia Britannica. https://www.britannica.com/topic/paganism

Wikipedia contributors. (2024a, April 1). *Shamanism - Wikipedia.* https://en.wikipedia.org/wiki/Shamanism#:~:text=Shamanism%20is%20a%20system%20of,the%20dead%20to%20the%20afterlife.

Wikipedia contributors. (2024b, April 29). *Paganism.* Wikipedia. https://en.wikipedia.org/wiki/Paganism#:~:text=Paganism%20(from%20classical%20Latin%20p%C4%81g%C4%81nus,ethnic%20religions%20other%20than%20Judais

Wikipedia contributors. (2024c, May 7). *Wicca.* Wikipedia. https://en.wikipedia.org/wiki/Wicca

Printed in Dunstable, United Kingdom

72245088R00080